Praise for *Look What You've Done*

"I love Tasha and her honesty, vulnerability, and absolute fire for Jesus. *Look What You've Done* will deepen your understanding of God and how he works in our lives. Grab one for you and anyone who needs a reminder that God uses each person's story for His glory!"

—Christy Nockels, worship leader and
bestselling author of *The Life You Long For*

"I've come to know and love Tasha like a sister. Not only have we had the privilege of sharing messages of hope through music to our audiences on stage, but also laughter and deep heart conversations off stage. Tasha is the real deal, and the more I've learned about her story, the more inspired I am by her incredible faith. The way that God has always been working in her life, challenges me to look at my own journey with new eyes. This is her story to honor what God has done, and I know it will inspire and challenge you, too!"

—Danny Gokey, Grammy and Dove
Award-winning Christian music artist,
and author of *Hope in Front of Me*

"Life is full of many battles. For my friend Tasha Layton, she has battled comparison, self-image, and the uncertainty of finding her purpose. She has fought with courage and that has been a huge encouragement to me. Through this journey, she has acquired so much wisdom to be passed down. This book is a testament to what God has done through her and her family.

—Jordan Feliz, Award-winning
musician and Singer-songwriter of #1
hit song, "Jesus is Coming Back"

"My friend Tasha loves Jesus in such a beautiful way. You will love her new book *Look What You've Done*, she shares some of the most powerful stories and provides intimate self-reflections on what God was doing along the way. God is at work in Tasha so hang in there on the ride to better see what God is doing in your life!"

—Jon Reddick, Dove Award-
nominated worship singer

"When we worship, we are meant to suspend our desires and give them to Jesus. This is what my friend, Tasha Layton, does in the way she sings and lives her life. She has lived quite a dramatic life. In *Look What You've Done*, her first full-length book, you'll see new ways to worship Jesus in your life."

—Chris McClarney, worship leader
and songwriter of the chart topping
song, "Your Love Never Fails"

LOOK WHAT YOU'VE DONE

Foreword by *New York Times*
Bestselling author, Bob Goff

LOOK
WHAT
YOU'VE
DONE

THE LIES WE BELIEVE
AND THE TRUTH
THAT SETS US FREE

TASHA LAYTON

with Jocelyn Bailey

FRANKLIN, TENNESSEE

K-LOVE BOOKS

5700 West Oaks Blvd.
Rocklin, CA 95765

Published by K-LOVE Books, an imprint of EMF Publishing, LLC, 5700 West Oaks Blvd, Rocklin, CA 95765.

ISBN: 978-1-954201-38-5
10 9 8 4 6 5 4 3 2 1

ISBN: 978-1-954201-38-5 (Hardcover)
ISBN: 978-1-954201-40-8 (Ebook)
ISBN: 978-1-954201-39-2 (Audio)
Publisher's Cataloging-in-Publication data

Names: Layton, Tasha, author.
Title: Look what you've done : the lies we believe & the truth that sets us free / Tasha Layton.
Description: Franklin, TN: K-Love, 2023.
Identifiers: ISBN: 978-1-954201-38-5 (hardcover) | 978-1-954201-40-8 (ebook) | 978-1-954201-39-2 (audio)
Subjects: LCSH Layton, Tasha. | Contemporary Christian musicians--United States--Biography. | Contemporary Christian musicians--Religious life. | Christian life. | Christian biography. | BISAC RELIGION / Christian Living. / Personal Growth. | BIOGRAPHY & AUTOBIOGRAPHY / Religious.
Classification: LCC ML420.L39 2023 | DDC 277.3/0825/092--dc23

Cover design by Thinkpen
Interior design by PerfecType, Nashville, TN

To the God who rescued me and turned my ashes to beauty—
May I always place my trust in You

CONTENTS

CONTENTS

FOREWORD

I have sailed across the Pacific a couple times. I'm not sure why I do it because I spend most of the time over the rail hurling. There are some positives of course—each trip is usually good for eliminating twenty to thirty pounds from around my waist. The hard part is watching other people eat real food you can't keep down and having to sleep below deck with a bunch of guys who haven't showered for a couple weeks. The trick to getting across the ocean is not only to fill your sails with wind, but to keep the kelp from wrapping around the keel. A strand of kelp can be hundreds of feet long and when it wraps around the keel it can slow you down to a crawl.

We all have certain beliefs and some of us play host to a few lies as well. Some beliefs and lies are our creations and others are borrowed. Lies are kelp; borrowed beliefs steal your wind. Together they conspire to slow you down and will take you off course. During our short lives, we have the opportunity to sort out the return address about things we have come to believe about ourselves, our friends, and our faith. We also can separate the lies we have believed from the truths we have held. If we don't do this important and courageous work, we will be left professing things we are not fully convinced of and acting certain about things we are only guessing about.

What Tasha has written in the pages that follow is an honest account of the events that shaped her, the faith she discovered, and the doubts she got real with. This book is an account of clearing the kelp from the keel on a journey worth taking. This is a tender and honest book about the power of truth and Jesus to displace the lies, mistruths, and false narratives we all have adopted to some degree along the way. As you turn the last page, you will realize that this book is your invitation to set sail with Jesus and actively participate in the adventure He has invited you to join, if you're willing to show up for it.

—*New York Times* bestselling author, Bob Goff

INTRODUCTION

I stood in a clearing, my eyes trained on the sun setting behind the Rocky Mountains in the distance. The colors swirling in the sky competed with the warmth of the sun's glare. I took a deep breath. Exhaled. The crisp Colorado air moved across my skin, sending goosebumps up and down my bare arms.

God, how did I get here?

I heard my counselor, Pete, rustling in the grass nearby. I had almost forgotten that he was the one who brought me up here.

"Is that not the most beautiful sunset you've ever seen?" he asked.

I nodded in response. As the sun inched ever closer to the horizon line, the colors continued to shift and deepen, an ever-moving landscape.

"As beautiful as that sunset is," Pete continued, "God thinks you are even more beautiful than that."

I took in his words and held them close for a moment. Then he asked me the crucial question:

"Do you believe it?"

His voice was calm and kind.

A lump swelled in my throat. *Did* I believe it? Was Pete right in saying I was beautiful to God? I knew what the scriptures said, but did I feel them in my heart? I *wanted* to see myself as God's beautiful child, a creature beloved and cherished by Him. But so many years of pain and lies had locked me up like a vault.

Do you believe it, Tasha?

I closed my eyes and prayed. *God, is it true? Am I beautiful in Your sight? This time, can I really and truly trust You? Am I worthy of Your love?*

My eyes opened. And as the sun's final glowing edge dipped below the mountain, something clicked into place.

* * *

That day in Colorado was a turning point for me, but so much had led up to it. I'd gone from faithful to fallen, successful to shamed, and all the way back again in a matter of years. We're talking low lows and really high highs. I'd traveled all over the world, met more people than I could count, and tried out almost every religion in the book. By the time I went to get help in Colorado, I'd exhausted my body and my mental resources. I believed I had nowhere else to go.

God intervened.

But I'm getting ahead of myself.

My name is Tasha, and you may already know me as a singer and a songwriter. Other people know me as a worship leader. Or you may not know me at all, and that's okay! I'm thrilled to meet you either way. In the last fifteen years, I've lived more than I ever thought I would and had unique experiences I couldn't have dreamed up for myself. I've also felt shame heavy enough to bury a soul and begged God to save me from the depths of despair.

These days, it's my great honor to sing and worship God and meet incredible people whose hearts long for healing. Some feel frustrated and constrained in their lives. Perhaps they've lived in the same zip code for years, or they feel like they're being held captive by an unrealized dream they carry in the unseen part of their soul. Their deepest desires are not met, and they are painfully aware of that fact.

Believe me when I say I've been there too.

Some people have trouble believing that God loves them or that His promises are available to them. Maybe they're battling fears, doubts, or suffering of their own.

For a long time, I wondered why God was withholding good things from me. I was confused and frustrated, and I couldn't hear His voice or understand what He was doing. Little did I know that He was working behind the scenes, accomplishing everything in His good and perfect time. As I've looked back at the turning points of my life, I can now see what He was up to—and I can only marvel at His powerful, precious plan for me.

A couple years ago, I released a song called "Look What You've Done," which inspired the title of this book. Like every song I write, it reflects my heart, and in many ways, it's the theme of my life so far. While the words at first confess the shame I've felt, the redeeming message is what God has done with the brokenness in my life. No matter what *I* do, God can turn it around. He's taken the things that once made me feel weak and turned them into my greatest strengths. I could never have done these things on my own; only God could have healed me from the inside out.

When I set out to write this book, I wanted to talk about what God had done in my life. Though I didn't even know it during my years of wandering, God was busy writing a beautiful story for me—and I am confident that God has an amazing adventure planned for each and every soul.

With God as the Master Planner, we can each have confidence in His unimaginably good plans. As Ephesians 2:10 reminds us, "We are God's handiwork, created in Christ Jesus to do good works, which God prepared in advance for us to do." How special are we that God not only made us but has dreams of His own for us? People who are really living life to the fullest are not angsty about their dreams; they are living in the belief that God is the Source of their hope.

As such, I hope you will step forward in the belief that your dreams are worthy of passion and courage. There's a special kind of alignment that happens when we listen for God and ask Him to show us the way. When our dreams sync up with His, amazing things will happen. If God can do it for me, He can do it for you. It was only when I loosened my stubborn grip that God was able to work in ways I never could have dreamed.

Your path is unique—beautiful and different from everyone's else's. My hope is that the stories I tell here will create points of connection between us, serving as reminders that we are all looking for freedom, hope, and joy. At the end of each chapter, I've also included a scripture and questions for reflection. I encourage you to make some quiet time for yourself because that's an effective way to listen for the Lord's voice. Perhaps as we walk through these stories together, you'll hear Him in the silence and realize He is near.

At the same time, I understand that sometimes God seems far away. I want to talk about those moments too—the moments when you're crying in your car and throwing out your plans and feeling like your life is never going to start. I'm not going to sugarcoat anything in these chapters because that never helped anyone. We need to be honest with ourselves and each other about our low moments too.

You're not alone in this world. You're not the only one who feels stuck. For so many years, I didn't see a path to freedom. But over time, I have come to see that God is with me on this journey. And guess what. He is with you too. Every single person's life can be a testament to God's power and love. He has done amazing things through the people who have entrusted their lives to Him. As God's children, we can all be creative and free.

My prayer is that you will find encouragement and strength in these pages. Together, let's discover a sense of God's presence and revel in the joy He provides. This book is not a how-to guide or a manual for living. What it is, however, is an example of a journey with all its challenges and triumphs. I like to think of it as bits and pieces of wisdom about navigating our paths while looking to God for direction. We learn about ourselves and God through every mountain and every valley.

God is good to everyone and has compassion on what He has made (Psalm 145:9). That includes you and me. Let's experience Him in a genuine way together. I can't wait to show you what God has already done and what He can still do.

Chapter 1

LESS-THAN

I grew up in a small, Southern town in South Carolina. We had a post office, a volunteer fire station, and one flashing light. Technically, the light belonged to the neighboring town, but we claimed it. It was the kind of place some people might call "backwoods." To me, it was just home.

My family was of humble means, and I had few friends at the time. This was in large part because my family couldn't afford sports teams, dance classes, or other social activities where kids tend to meet and make friends. We also lived in a trailer on acreage out in the country, far away from a neighborhood, and I never felt comfortable asking classmates over because I knew our house wasn't as nice as theirs. You probably won't be surprised to hear that I was called "trailer trash" more than once in my life.

At a young age, I learned—or decided—that people in "normal" houses were better than me. It's truly amazing how even little children can accept these damaging ideas as truth. The reality was, I grew up in a mostly loving environment and Christian home—much healthier than some of my peers—and my family was trying hard to be fiscally responsible. My parents are both extremely hard workers who did their best, and I would not change a thing about my early life. But those facts did not stop people from judging or stop me from feeling less-than.

Like so many girls, I also thought I wasn't pretty enough. Specifically, I didn't have the right hairstyle and hairbows. When I look back at old yearbooks, I can't help but laugh at how silly these trendy hairstyles were, but you couldn't have explained that to me then. All I knew was that I didn't own a single hairbow, and I had a mom who didn't know how to braid.

My mom was a bit of a tomboy type back then. Instead of making brownies for PTA bake sales, she spent her time taking me trail riding and target shooting in her jeep. Instead of fetching me from cheerleading practice in a minivan, she picked me up from the art club on a motorcycle. Some of the kids and teachers may have thought this was cool, but I was mortified! What I wanted was a mom who flew under the radar—someone who looked and acted like everyone else.

I am grateful now for how my childhood shaped me, but back then, all I understood was what I *didn't* have. Rejection was painful, so I sought to never give anyone a reason to think I was inferior or less-than. This was when the seeds of perfectionism and performance were planted in me, and before long, they took root. I would pretend to be whatever I needed to be so people wouldn't think less of me—and as a result, I didn't feel safe to be myself around anyone.

> I didn't yet understand that the real Tasha—the one God created—is the perfect original.

In one way or another, I think most children and adolescents experience this desire to fit in. But I remember losing total track of who I was. I didn't yet understand that the real Tasha—the one God created—is the perfect original. It has taken me years to get there. And sadly, some people never escape this mindset. They spend their lives trying to accommodate some phony ideal, never giving God a chance to celebrate them for who they are.

Comparison is a disease in our world, maybe now more than ever. It robs people of identity, contentment, and joy. Focusing on what you *don't* have or what you *haven't* accomplished makes it nearly impossible to celebrate the things you *do* have. As we scroll through our social media feeds and take in photoshopped images of "perfect" lives, we forget to be grateful for the blessings already in our pockets. You can spend your whole life wanting to look better and have more things, but no one will find happiness in that sort of endless wanting.

When we spin our wheels trying to be someone else, it's usually because we haven't yet let God tell us who we are. We are so uniquely fashioned as humans, and no two people are exactly alike. Psalm 139:14 tells us we are "fearfully and wonderfully made." Our very fingerprints are physical reminders of our distinct individuality. And yet, we all have them—which speaks to our collective nature as God's beloved creation. The fact that we were made with care by the Creator of the universe should give us confidence beyond measure. How special does it make you feel to know that God crafted you and breathed life into you, and He will never do it the same way ever again?

I think back to my childhood and how lucky I was to have parents who loved and cared for me. Maybe *grateful* is a better word than *lucky*. To people who didn't know any better, maybe I seemed like trailer trash. But I was deeply cherished and cared for. *That* was the truth of my identity—not some label put on me by judgmental outsiders. I'm so thankful now for what I know were blessings, even if I didn't fully understand it then. Yes, maybe my mother did me wrong by giving me a bowl cut in the second grade, but that's a story for another time. Despite that egregious offense, I know she loved me.

Until we start practicing gratitude for what we have and who God made us to be, we may never be able to truly accomplish what our hearts are made for. And yet, I know self-acceptance is an easy thing to talk about in theory but not an easy thing to actually do. If you're feeling like you've lost track of yourself and who you are in Christ, I encourage you to take a few moments now to talk to God. Ask Him to remind you who you are and what makes you special in His eyes. Ask Him to help you make gratitude your default perspective.

> Until we start practicing gratitude for what we have and who God made us to be, we may never be able to truly accomplish what our hearts are made for.

And after you've done that, spend a little time talking to Him about your dreams. What are the desires of your heart, and are they in alignment with what God wants for you? I believe these conversations with God are the only way we can break the chain of comparison and finally find peace in who He created us to be.

Together, let's stop trying to copy people who are putting on a performance rather than living their truest lives. Let's stop trying to squeeze ourselves into molds that weren't made for us—even the wonky-shaped molds we've fashioned for ourselves. Our beautiful, unique, handmade identities are in God alone, and may we never lose sight of Him as the One who carries our dreams. With Him as the Author of our lives, we will never fail by comparison.

I have loved you with an everlasting love;
therefore I have continued my faithfulness to you.
—Jeremiah 31:3 ESV

QUESTIONS TO CONSIDER

1. Can you remember a moment from your childhood when you were made to feel less-than? How did that experience carry over into your adult life?
2. What are some things you are especially grateful for today?
3. How does it feel to know that you are God's handiwork—and that no one who's ever lived can compare to you?

Chapter 2

WILD & FREE

When I was a teenager, my parents gave me a rescue horse named Lady for my birthday. Yes, it's true, I was a horse girl. It's practically a requirement for Southern girls to love horses.

Lady, a red horse with dark red hair and a white star on her forehead, was a Thoroughbred and quarter horse mix who had been severely abused. And let me tell you: she was feisty. She seemed to have an extra amount of fight in her, probably due to what she'd been through. Honestly, I think she might've been a little off, and she was known for bucking people off from time to time. She was wild and free and made her own rules—which was why I loved her but was afraid of her at the same time.

When I rode Lady, I was mostly in control, but her stubbornness was hard for me to handle. (Have I mentioned that I love being in charge? I've been this way a long time.) Yet part of me related to her nature. Like her, I was always up for an adventure. And while she was fighting her demons, I was fighting to figure out who my true self was. For someone who'd never had a real riding lesson in her life, I'd like to think I did a pretty good job holding my own with Lady.

We had many acres—part pasture, part creek, part yard, and part garden or land used for farming. I was a country girl, usually running around half-clothed in the dirt outside. Part of our land I was familiar with, and Lady and I had worn a path in the dirt from riding around the pastures. But my gutsy side always had a hankering to venture beyond the fence, and I longed to venture out yet was a little scared of what Lady might do.

Then one day, curiosity got hold of me and overpowered the fear. Maybe it got hold of us both. Anyway, I rode her past the boundaries of the property on our land. As we crossed the fence line onto untrodden paths, Lady seemed unsure. Her ears spun and her eyes bugged out as she took inventory of all the new territory around her. I let out the breath I'd been holding. We'd officially stepped out and ventured into the wild unknown.

What happened next caused my life to flash before my eyes. My whole body jolted, and we were off. Lady decided she was free and started running as fast as she could. Any sort of control I'd thought I had was now officially gone, *adios*, goodbye. Not only did she tear past our property line, but she continued across a highway and into a neighboring pasture. Amid a stream of words I won't repeat, I cried out for God's mercy, thinking I was a goner. I think I have blocked some of this wild ride from my memory!

Yet I didn't block it *all* out. At some point my eyes refocused and landed on the pastures all around us—landscapes I had never seen. They were gorgeous and rolling and entirely new to me. For a few seconds the terror subsided, and I felt the thrill of the ride and the peace of total surrender. I no longer feared what she could do to me but gave in completely to the rush of the moment. Together, Lady and I were blazing a new trail.

Eventually, my soul returned to my body, and I realized we were slowing down. Maybe God was answering my prayer, or maybe Lady was just out of shape and needed to catch her breath. Either way, we both survived. I don't even remember how we made it back home; I just remember that we did. Something directed us back toward familiar fields and the trodden path of the home pasture.

This wild ride taught me a few things. For one, I knew for certain now that Lady was something I wasn't in charge of! But even more, the whole experience helped me to better understand that losing control isn't the worst thing in the world. In fact, fear of losing control can hold us back, preventing us from seeing the gorgeous green pastures beyond the gates of our known worlds. Horses are meant to run wild and free sometimes. And so are you and I.

Truth is, even when we stayed within the boundaries of our land, I never had full control over Lady. She was always her own girl, an untamed spirit. And though we may cling to the illusion of control in our own lives, it won't take long for God to remind us who's *really* holding the reins. Only the God of the heavens, who made "all the heavenly bodies by the breath of his mouth," decides what the future holds (Psalm 33:6 ISV). Yet when we answer His call to freedom, handing over the reins and surrendering our plans to Him, we may just be opening the gate to the wildest, most exhilarating ride of our lives.

> Losing control isn't the worst thing in the world.

Over the years, I've learned to welcome thrills in the most literal sense. Lady's wild ride was only the start. People seem shocked when I tell them I've been bungee jumping and skydiving multiple times—to the point that I was almost declined a life insurance policy. The first time I jumped out of a plane, it was on the Gold Coast of Australia. It was such a beautiful sight that I jumped out of another plane in Dubai. Then I took my now-husband, Keith, skydiving on a date. I've hang-glided, learned to scuba dive, and backpacked across countries on my own. And every time I embrace the uncertainty of a journey, I find myself encountering people, feelings, and experiences only God could have put in my path.

Loosening my grip (or giving up some control) is a lesson God is still teaching me every day. When I'm faced with misgivings or a situation that makes me feel vulnerable, my instinct is to try to manage God rather than trust Him. But every time I do step out in faith, even just a few steps beyond the boundary, I remember the thrill of surrender. It feels like peace and excitement all at once, knowing my God is big enough to steer my course. He's in charge of my relationships, my

> And every time I embrace the uncertainty of a journey, I find myself encountering people, feelings, and experiences only God could have put in my path.

parenting, my career, and everything else in this big, wide universe. And though He may need to remind me of it sometimes, I know He's worthy of my trust.

The journey might steal your breath or even stop your heart—but you will never forget the rush of a life truly surrendered.

> *Now the Lord is the Spirit, and where the*
> *Spirit of the Lord is, there is freedom.*
> —2 Corinthians 3:17

QUESTIONS TO CONSIDER

1. Try to think of a time when you felt truly unbridled and free. What prompted the feeling, and what made that moment so special?

2. Describe something that scares you. Where do you think that fear came from? Is it a healthy fear, or is it a fear worth conquering?

3. Why is it so difficult to hand over the reins of our lives to God? What are we afraid of losing?

Chapter 3

TAMBOURINES

Though my family had raised me Southern Baptist, we started attending an Assemblies of God church when I was about eight years old. To a kid, this meant switching from a quiet church to a louder church! I'll never forget our first visit: colorful banners adorned the walls, and a woman sang her heart out with a tambourine. I thought, *They play tambourines here? Have I hit the jackpot?* I had never seen anything like it.

Everyone seemed so happy to be together in that place, thankful for the privilege of worship. I suppose the best word to describe it would be *alive*. Joy, gratitude, and excitement filled the air, to the point that even a child could sense God's presence. To this day, I think about that church as the place where expressions of faith became fully real to me. In the book of Jeremiah, God says, "I've never quit loving you and never will. Expect love, love, and more love! . . . You'll resume your singing, grabbing tambourines and joining the dance" (31:3–4 MSG). That verse came fully to life before my eyes as I looked around from my seat and hoped desperately for the kind of joy I witnessed.

> To this day, I think about that church as the place where expressions of faith became fully real to me.

Music had already become a big part of my life. If you need video evidence, my parents still have VHS tapes of me singing into a hairbrush while my grandmother played guitar. I was mesmerized by her playing and by anyone who could coax music out of an instrument. Most of the people in my family were musical, so I never lacked an opportunity to listen. What a blessing it was to be born into such a music-filled home.

Aside from my musical performances, I would dress up and put on cheesy plays with my sister, Shannon. We're talking full sets, scripts, costumes—total blackmail material. Creative play came naturally to me, and I adored my music and art teachers in school. So you can imagine how thrilling it was to discover that church could be a place for me to express my creative side in worship. By the time I was a teenager, I was singing solos on Sunday mornings.

Performing in public didn't come all that easily, though. Moments before I was supposed to sing, my nerves would get the best of me to the point of sickness. I'd picture myself forgetting the words, missing a note, or embarrassing myself in some as-yet-unimagined-but-somehow-still-terrifying way. Then I'd race to the bathroom, vomit, and race back to the front of the church. I got sick of being sick. I wanted to sing, but not like this. Over time I learned some tricks for calming my nerves— such as writing the lyrics between my index finger and thumb, in a spot where I could see the words while holding a microphone—but nothing ever completely chased away the fear.

Then one Sunday, while standing in my typical circle of jitters, it occurred to me to ask God for help. I closed my eyes and prayed, *God, please help me overcome this fear. I'm just so tired of it.* And almost before that prayer had fully formed in my mind, I heard a still, small voice whisper, *It's not about you, Tasha.*

Sometimes things just click in your soul, mind, and body all at once. I realized there were people who needed to hear the words I was going to sing. Singing in church had never been about my talent or my perfect delivery; it was about the One I was singing for and about.

God didn't and still doesn't need my abilities. He's God! What He desired was my heart. My motivation was the thing that needed to change, and once that became clear to me, my worries and hang-ups all seemed to dissipate. That short prayer, little more than a passing plea in my mind, unlocked everything for me.

I sang with everything I had that Sunday. I didn't sing flawlessly, but I sang without any regard for myself. Serving the people I was singing to and stewarding well the gift God had given me was the point. Since entering the music industry, I still deal with bouts of nervousness, but those moments are few and far between now. To be able to sing about God without worrying about an audience judging me harshly is the most freeing feeling imaginable—as if I've stepped right into the purpose He set out for me.

Whatever you're afraid of, I guarantee God can help you overcome it. Maybe what you do each day has nothing to do with public performance, but you find yourself paralyzed by how you're being perceived. I've experienced this firsthand, and I think we all battle these fears, worries, and insecurities by nature. But if you're feeling held back, shackled by the thought of what others might think of you, ask God to remove this burden. You may not receive an immediate answer, but God is not in the business of fear. He's in the business of courage, and He wants you to feel bold and free. I wish everyone on earth could feel the weight of fear falling off their shoulders and the pleasure of going forth without such a heavy burden.

Remember the lady with the tambourine I mentioned? Well, let's just say she made quite the impression on me. She was having such a good time, worshiping God without a care in the world, and I wanted a part of it. That Sunday we came home after church, and I decided I needed a tambourine of my own. "Can I have a tambourine for Christmas?" I asked. "Please? Pretty please?"

> God is not in the business of fear. He's in the business of courage.

Eventually I got one, and I have it to this day. It reminds me of that precious time—the days of my life when I learned what it means to sing to God with joy.

Rejoice in the Lord always. I will say it again: Rejoice!
Let your gentleness be evident to all. The Lord is
near. Do not be anxious about anything, but in every
situation, by prayer and petition, with thanksgiving,
present your requests to God. And the peace of God,
which transcends all understanding, will guard
your hearts and your minds in Christ Jesus.
—Philippians 4:4–7

QUESTIONS TO CONSIDER

1. Have you ever met someone who seems fully free and fully surrendered to God? Describe this person. What characterizes his or her life?
2. What is something you have always wanted to do but have been afraid to try?
3. What, if any, creative forms of expression appeal to you? Why do you think God made us with creative hearts and minds?

Chapter 4

CHIA PET

When I was five or six years old, I had a nightmare. I can't recall many details—only that it was terrifying and evil. When I woke up, I was so scared and ashamed that I didn't tell anyone about it. My brain at that tender age decided that because my own thoughts had conjured up the horrible images, I was most likely an innately bad person. Only an evil mind could've come up with such a dream, I reckoned.

The dream was a secret I kept locked away until I was an adult. In fact, I didn't speak about it to anyone until I met my counselor, Pete, in Colorado twenty-five years later. I now know that dreams can be caused by so many things: existing fears, poor sleep environments, bad pizza, and so on. But I didn't know that as a kid. For years that dream haunted me, as did the conclusion I drew from it. The unspoken belief that I was a bad, unworthy, defective person took deep root in my young heart.

Around this time, I also went through something at school so humiliating that it reinforced this hideous belief. I was in first grade, and we were taking turns practicing reading out loud. Well before it would have been my turn, nature called. I raised my hand and asked to go to the bathroom, knowing I'd be able to go to the little girls' room and return in a flash.

My teacher assumed I was trying to get out of my turn, so she flatly told me no.

"You'll take your turn reading just like everyone else," she said.

So I waited for a few more minutes. I *really* had to pee, so I raised my hand again. The teacher told me no once more, though my situation was growing more urgent. I think I asked her four times total, only to be told no each time.

When it was finally my turn to read, I was miserable. I stood up, walked to the front of the classroom, and began to read. Within seconds, I felt the warmth running down my legs. I couldn't stop it, and it became clear to everyone in front of me what was happening. The other students began to howl with laughter at me standing there, huge wet spots blooming all over my pants. I looked at my teacher, desperate for help.

You'd think a teacher would take pity on me and my situation, but not this teacher. Seemingly annoyed by the mess and the distraction I'd caused, she told me to go wait in the bathroom in the back of the classroom. I rushed in and slammed the door, sinking to the floor in embarrassment.

I sat there for hours, and no one came to help me. For the rest of the day, I cried and sat in my wet clothes, wondering why my teacher was punishing me like this. My mind spun and spun as I waited and waited. When she finally opened the door, it was time to go home. By the time I got there, kids had already left messages on our family's answering machine making fun of me.

> Maybe I really *was* a bad child who deserved such treatment.

It's even hard for me as an adult to reckon with what happened that day. As a parent with little kids who make messes all the time, I can't imagine what would motivate an adult to do something like what was done to me. But when I was little, the only thing I understood was shame. Maybe I really *was* a bad child who deserved such treatment. No other explanation made sense.

* * *

Even smaller incidents stick with you. By the time I was in sixth grade, I had a fully formed understanding of myself as less-than, though I had grown a bit more independent despite it. Then one day I sat down in class, only for a boy to turn around, give me a once-over, and start chanting, "Ch-ch-ch-chiaaaaaa!"

Now, readers of a certain age will know that he was singing the jingle to a fad product known as the Chia Pet. For younger readers, let me just tell you that the Chia Pet took the nineties by storm. It was this strange terracotta toy that you watered and then chia seeds sprouted and grew out of it like hair. If you still can't picture it, go and Google it. It'll be like opening a time capsule to the twentieth century.

Anyway, the boy was trying to make a joke about my hair—that is, my *leg* hair. Unbeknownst to me, girls at that age had started to shave their legs, while I was blithely living the hairy-legs life. As kids around me laughed with him, I felt that familiar mortification. Part of being that age is being embarrassed all the time, but I didn't even know until that moment what I was supposed to be embarrassed about.

I went home, determined to never let this boy make fun of me again. I was going to shave my legs. I did not ask for any help. I have always been the self-reliant type, to say the least. I locked the bathroom door so no one could find me and proceeded to shave my legs in the way I imagined it should go.

Well, I soon found out that shaving one's legs isn't about pressing down as hard as possible on the skin. A short while and a bathroom floor covered in blood later, I still have the scar. Screaming and crying ensued as my sister (rightly) made fun of me and my mom bandaged me up. To top it all off, I obviously didn't even finish the job! I wore pants to school for a while to hide my partially hairy, partially shaven, partially wounded right leg. What an absolute mess.

* * *

I share all these stories not for pity, but because I am willing to bet you have similar ones! The things that happen to us when we are young are interesting to therapists for a reason: because the memories inform who we eventually become. Our little minds don't know how to cope with some information, and the result can be so damaging.

The Enemy is good at seizing upon lies and misunderstandings and reinforcing them as truths. Jesus Himself described the Enemy as "the father of lies" (John 8:44).

This Enemy will happily use even the smallest painful incident and turn it into lasting harm.

A loneliness I wouldn't be able to uproot for many years established itself in my young heart. As wounded as I felt from kids calling me names for superficial reasons, I couldn't bear the thought of being rejected for just being who I was—so it was much easier to be a false version of Tasha. Being vulnerable or letting anyone see the real me meant risking rejection of the *real* me, and that was not a risk worth taking.

> Being vulnerable or letting anyone see the real me meant risking rejection of the *real* me, and that was not a risk worth taking.

I also had begun to believe that the true version of myself wasn't worth getting to know. Thoughts of that childhood dream nagged me, reminding me that I was unworthy, unlovable, maybe even unfixable. Deep down in my heart, I believed that something serious was wrong with me. It was so much easier to hide, to present a version of myself that would please others and conceal my shameful parts. I had no idea yet of what I looked like to God, my Father. All I could feel was humiliation.

In a few chapters, I'll talk more about my healing journey at a counseling facility in Colorado. But for now, I hope you'll take a few moments to think about your own past. What do you recall from your youth that may have informed your understanding of yourself? Sometimes an experience doesn't seem all that bad in hindsight, but our immediate response and understanding of it has yielded lasting trauma. Whatever your story, pray over it with God and ask Him to root out the lies you've believed. He is the only one who can replace the lies, and He will fill you up with truth.

> *Jesus said, "If you hold to my teaching, you are really my disciples. Then you will know the truth, and the truth will set you free."*
> —John 8:31–32

QUESTIONS TO CONSIDER

1. What is a lie about yourself that you believed as a child and then carried into adulthood? What impact did it have on your life?

2. Think back to a moment when you felt humiliated. What happened, and how did it make you feel about yourself?

3. When have you felt pressured to be a false version of yourself? What were your reasons, and what were the outcomes?

Chapter 5

DERAILED

Our church in South Carolina was the place where I grew in faith, fell deeper in love with music, and discovered my passion for worship. When I was thirteen years old and at a youth conference in Florida, I felt the first true call on my life. Jeanne Mayo was speaking, and as she spoke with confidence and power, I saw God in who she was. As I sat in my seat, my heart nearly beat out of my chest when she spoke out to those of us who felt called to ministry. She asked us to join her up front for prayer, and at those words, I jumped up and bolted from the balcony all the way to the front! It was an emotional altar moment for me. I'll never forget that Steven Curtis Chapman's "For the Sake of the Call" was playing as I made my way down the aisle. God's work in me had already begun.

By the time I was in high school, I was even more dedicated to my faith. My spiritual practices were serious and sincere, to the point that I often fasted, prayed, and read my Bible for hours at a time after school. Whenever the church doors were open, I was inside. I tried to make good decisions and stayed away from the drinking, sex, and other bad habits teenagers often take part in. And while part of this was about true devotion to God's instruction for me, I know now that another part of my rigor was about proving to myself and others that I was good enough to deserve God's love and mercy.

People who looked at me when I was sixteen probably believed I was a healthy and thriving young Christian. I certainly looked the part. I was still active in my youth group and singing with the worship team on Sundays, and I had even begun dating the pastor's son. He was also on the worship team, and we made sense together. Though I really cared for him, little did I know that our relationship was doomed. In no way could I have predicted the devastation to follow and the harm it would do to my heart, my faith, and my understanding of the church.

* * *

Being a public person is a challenge, whether you are a person of faith or not. The pressure you feel to perform can be as exhilarating as it can be crushing. Though I've learned so much over the years about how to balance the public's expectations with the goal of my music—to worship God and glorify Him to the fullest—those tender, young years of singing in church were incredibly vulnerable ones. I had no tools for dealing with what others thought of me, and I was deeply susceptible to their criticisms. They consumed me and derailed my faith for years—years when I wandered and grieved and almost gave up on God. And it all started with my boyfriend's mother.

The young man I sang with on the worship team was good to me, but for reasons I cannot fully explain, his mother did not see me as a fitting partner for her son. She made her opinion known to me as she chastised me in public, but even more, she made wild accusations about me to other members of the church. As a leader herself—the wife of a pastor—she held lots of sway with the congregants, and before long, rumors swirled about my character. She accused me of seducing her son, embodying an evil spirit, and ultimately trying to split the entire church. None of these rumors were true, but they were destructive nonetheless. As a self-conscious teenager, I had no idea how to respond to her accusations or the anonymous letters that arrived at my house and seemed to confirm what she saw in me. She looked at me and told me, "You only sing for yourself, Tasha. You're not doing this for God." Before long, I was removed from my position on the worship team.

Much later, I learned that this wounded woman had a troubling past of her own that might have led to such behavior, but I doubt this knowledge would have changed much for me at the time. The damage had already been done. Not only had my lifelong dream of leading worship been destroyed, but my heart had been wrecked from the inside out. The idea that I was evil and unworthy of singing in church sent me all the way back to my childhood dream—I was convinced that something was horribly wrong with me. Echoes of that dream appeared in the hateful words she used against me.

Even though I knew the accusations she made were lies, I internalized some of her sentiments and began to wonder again if I was, in fact, an evil person. Young people are so liable to this thinking—accepting others' judgments as true when there are no facts whatsoever to back them up. All the same, I was devastated. The community where I'd once found God had unceremoniously decided I wasn't worthy of their presence.

I know I'm not the only one who has been traumatized by experiences in the church. If you have a similar story, my heart goes out to you, and please hear me when I say you're not alone. I hate that I know what it feels like to be broken by people who are supposed to welcome and love you unconditionally, and I hate that you know it too. Churches are full of imperfect people, all of whom need God's redeeming presence every day. I just pray you will be able to see beyond the imperfection of humankind and set your heart on the One who can pull you out of the muck and the mire.

It's easier for me now to look back and see how unfair it was for an adult to act the way my boyfriend's mother did—let alone toward a teenager. That hindsight is a gift to me today, and I'm grateful to have it. But it took me many, many years to get here. It has taken prayer, therapy, searching, and long stretches of time when I thought God had abandoned me. Though I had accepted the lie that I wasn't good enough to earn God's grace, He had *already* given that grace to me. There was nothing to prove to Him because God gives of Himself to every person who believes in Him.

Despite the pain of that time, I'm still returning to the deep well God dug for me during my teenage years—the years when my thirst for Him was earnest, pure, and real. Even when my dreams appeared shattered on the ground before me, God was building something bigger in the background. I was already on a path to redemption even though I could only see the wreckage.

Recently, more than twenty years later, I attended the K-LOVE Fan Awards and had the privilege of singing at a songwriters' night with Cory Asbury, Mac Powell, Matt Maher, and Steven Curtis Chapman—all wonderful songwriters in the CCM (contemporary Christian music) world. Before we went onstage, I had a moment to share with Steven my story about what his song "For the Sake of the Call" meant to me. He was so kind and humble about it. Then I told him, "But if you sing that song tonight while we're out there, please sing it at the end. Just the thought of it will make me cry—and I need to keep it together if I'm going to keep singing!"

Well, so much for that. Not only did he sing it, but he sang it *to* me—*for* me—right in the middle of the performance. Of course, I couldn't be upset at him because I was so touched. Not for the first time, something from my past had come completely full circle. God had taken my childhood dream and shown me what only He could do with it. He had carried me through the hard places and made the most of my pain. And I knew He was not, and is not, done with me yet.

> *I therefore, a prisoner for the Lord, urge you to walk in a manner worthy of the calling to which you have been called, with all humility and gentleness, with patience, bearing with one another in love, eager to maintain the unity of the Spirit in the bond of peace. There is one body and one Spirit—just as you were called to the one hope that belongs to your call—one Lord, one faith, one baptism, one God and Father of all, who is over all and through all and in all.*
> —Ephesians 4:1–6 ESV

QUESTIONS TO CONSIDER

1. Have you dealt with an experience at church that derailed your faith? How did you move forward from it?
2. If someone has said something harmful to or about you, how long did those words stay in your heart?
3. Do you have a sense of your calling from God? If not, have you asked God to reveal it to you?

Chapter 6

THE SEARCH

After everything that happened at my home church, I was brokenhearted and needed to escape—so I left for college at age seventeen. Though my heart was hurting, the full extent of what happened hadn't yet set in. That's something I've since learned about traumatic experiences: they hide out in your heart and make themselves at home in ways you cannot always predict.

I started out as a music major because I was still hopeful that I could use music to serve God. Since I didn't have much of a traditional music education, I jumped in headfirst and tried to catch up with the other music majors at my college. Then almost two years in, I encountered the hurdle of advanced music theory. The learning curve was so steep that I found myself at a crisis point.

Time had not healed the wounds of my church trauma. If anything, I was more depressed, isolated, and emotionally distraught than ever, and the coursework pulled everything from the past to the surface. Voices and accusations still haunted me, tainting my feelings for something that had once brought me great joy and satisfaction.

You only sing for yourself, Tasha.

You care more about music than worship.

Though my heart wrestled with the truth, the lies won out. I knew that if people wanted to believe I had led worship for selfish reasons, then one surefire way to prove them wrong would be to let it go entirely. So I gave up music—locked it up and threw away the key with only a couple of music classes remaining toward my degree. I changed my major to religion and decided to study my way back to God.

So much of this was a façade, of course. You, too, may know what it's like to struggle with feelings you are ashamed to talk about. As I tried so hard to play the part of a strong Christian, I felt too embarrassed to share my doubts and fears with the world. So I hid my true self—pretending everything in my life was "just fine"—and grew more and more depressed. Where was God in all of this? Had He gone completely silent? Sensing all my remaining confidence slipping away, I withdrew further and further into myself.

These days I understand how depression works—that it drives the sufferer toward isolation. We fear our messiness will be too much for other people, especially other Christians who appear to be doing "just fine" themselves. So instead of telling the truth, we hide. We fear judgment from people whose faith lives are intact, who appear to be walking the Christian path without incident. In my case, I still feared that people would see right through me—that they would agree with the woman from my church who had identified an evil spirit within me. It was so much easier to hole up in my dorm room and avoid the criticism of others, so I'd turn off the lights and pull the covers up over my head. Maybe I deserved the darkness.

> We fear judgment from people whose faith lives are intact, who appear to be walking the Christian path without incident.

* * *

The Enemy's lies continued to do their dirty work on my spirit. Though I had once believed in God's love for me, my entire reality had changed. Not only was I disgusted with myself, but I was disgusted with myself for *trying* to act normal when not one thing was right within me. I even despised myself for feeling like I needed God's help! It's not too much to say that I fully hated myself in those moments, and I believed everyone else, maybe even God, hated me too. Those vicious thoughts moved through my mind on a loop. *I deserve to be miserable*, I despaired. *All I think about is myself. Maybe I don't even deserve to live.*

This part of my life is hard to talk about, but today I'm a firm believer in the idea that the most honest, vulnerable parts of a story are the most helpful to others. I'm not afraid of the ugly, messy truth anymore, so here I go.

One day, alone in my dorm room, I tried to end it all. By then I was so numb to existence that ending my life felt like a rational decision. *I might even be doing the world a favor*, I figured. As I sat there with a loaded gun, I longed for escape. I closed my eyes, raised the barrel to my temple, and pressed on the trigger. I took one more deep breath, thinking it would be my last.

The door sprang open, though I thought I had locked it. A friend stumbled in, and I dropped the gun in my hand. Seconds later, and they would have been too late.

I began to sob as it dawned on them the dire place I was in. I wish I could say that all my troubles evaporated right then. The reality that God had saved me from myself took a long time to take root in my heart, while the Enemy's lies about my worthlessness had already made themselves at home. But I will be forever grateful for the intervention that day. I didn't know how much life I still had to live, but escaping that low moment set me on a different course.

> The reality that God had saved me from myself took a long time to take root in my heart.

After my attempt on my own life, I was basically catatonic. I could barely move and needed some quick intervention, so I went down to Charleston, South Carolina, to stay with a former youth pastor's family. They welcomed me into their home and didn't expect me to do anything but heal. They didn't force me to talk but waited for me to process what had happened. As they loved me and took care of me, I began to recover. Though I still had a lot of wrestling to do, I had made it through the lowest point of the valley.

If you hear nothing else I have to say in this book, I hope you will hear this: The Enemy will tell you every lie imaginable to bring you to your knees. He will whisper in your ear that you are unlovable, useless, and undeserving of life. If given the chance, he will convince you that you have nothing to offer this world.

But I'm here to tell you that not one of those lies is true. God loves you more than you can possibly understand, and He wants you to *live*. He wants to be your refuge, your "stronghold in the time of trouble" (Psalm 37:39 ESV). And He wants to rescue you from any notion that you aren't loved. *You* are *loved. Your life matters. You are God's. You mean everything in the world to Him.*

Though I didn't quite believe it yet, I was on my way.

* * *

During school I had stopped going to church, having lost confidence in my long-held beliefs. I still didn't know where God was exactly, but I knew He wasn't showing Himself to me in the ways I expected Him to. So, ever the diligent student, I spent my college semesters and the summers in between searching for God in other places. I studied Hinduism, Jainism, and other world religions in classrooms and between the covers of textbooks. On two occasions, I traveled to Europe to study mysticism. I was sort of on my own *Eat, Pray, Love* journey—one set in motion by what felt like a breakup with my faith. Maybe if I searched long and hard enough, the world would provide me with answers. No matter what, I was determined to find them.

One of my favorite stopovers was Italy. If you've ever been there, seen pictures of the country, or eaten an authentic Italian dinner, you know it's not a hard place to love. Amid the operas, the cooking classes, and the language courses, I found my spirit coming back to life. Sometimes I would hop on a train or bus just to see where it would take me! But do you know what really surprised me about Italy? The nuns.

One night in Rome, I attended Vespers (an evening prayer service) at a small convent on the side of the city opposite the Vatican. Though I'd sworn off music myself, I was enraptured by the way the nuns chanted and sang in worship. Their secluded lifestyle fascinated me; I felt like they had figured out something I hadn't.

Being cloistered, these nuns never left their convent. *Never.* In all my searching, I was looking for truth strong enough to motivate me to do something like that. Could I imagine staying within the walls of one building for the remainder of my life—for God? The nuns dedicated every aspect of their lives to worshiping their Creator. And despite the obvious differences between the nuns and me, I felt such a camaraderie with them. Even in that moment, when I felt so far away from God, I longed for their kind of incredible, lifelong devotion.

There's a quotation long attributed to St. Catherine of Siena that goes something like this: "Be who God meant you to be, and you will set the world on fire." That sentiment grabbed me then as it does now. As I prepared to leave Italy and come home, I realized that the journey had given me some time to heal and the distance I needed to look for God without judgment. As I'd wandered the ancient streets, tasting new gelato flavors and pondering the mysteries of existence, I felt free to make mistakes and ask questions without people looking over my shoulder. No, I hadn't quite found God yet, but I was getting closer. Finding God would mean finding myself—and I would not stop until I found us both.

> Finding God would mean finding myself—and I would not stop until I found us both.

He brought them out of darkness, the utter darkness,
and broke away their chains.
Let them give thanks to the LORD for his unfailing love
and his wonderful deeds for mankind,
for he breaks down gates of bronze
and cuts through bars of iron.
—Psalm 107:14–16

QUESTIONS TO CONSIDER

1. In your lowest moments, how did you perceive God's presence? Did you long to find Him in the darkness? Be honest about your answer.
2. Have you ever tried to stack Jesus up against the rest of the world's gods and religions? What did you discover amid your search?
3. What does it feel like to be far away from God? Do you have any habits or practices that include inviting Him into your heart?

Chapter 7

THE RETURN

One of the rewards of the Christian life is being able to experience full-circle moments: when you look around and realize that the past has led you to the present, and God has been the Author of it all. I'm not saying everything will make sense in its time—some things only God can explain—but nothing compares to the exhilaration I feel when I can look around and say, "Look at what God has done here!"

After God saved me from myself, I slowly made my way back to Him. As He breathed life back into my aching heart, it became clear to me that Jesus—not any of the other faiths I'd explored—was the one path to God that had truly transformed my life and given me hope to survive. What I had noticed about the other religions I studied was a constant striving toward something—whether it be God, righteousness, enlightenment, or nothingness. Christianity, however, was God's pursuit of humankind. In Scripture, God's love seemed to chase people down. The other faiths I studied did not have such power in them. Though I found pieces of truth or peace in other religions, Christianity presented the kind of power to which no other faith tradition could compare.

It felt right to come home to the faith that had inspired my youth—the only spirituality that had been real and life-changing for me. When I pondered going back to church, returning to the place where so many traumatic things had occurred seemed like the wrong step. So I found a church more than an hour away, where I knew no one and no one knew me. I was determined to make it work.

It would be wrong of me to lie here and say that going back to church was easy. Though I had a clean slate with a new congregation, every Sunday for some time was a slog. I didn't feel the way I once had about worship, which was frustrating and disheartening. Yet I resolved to keep going anyway, taking a step in pure faith and hoping that something would eventually "stick."

Sometimes faith is about making choices like this, I've learned. My study of Judaism inspired this belief; I admired the Jews' commitment to obedience, which is demonstrated by both the Old Testament and current-day Jewish practices. I thought that maybe if I resolved to walk by faith and not by sight, something would change in my soul. I needed to find my joy again, even if by sheer force of will.

Before long, my heart caught up with my choice.

One Sunday morning, the pastor said to us, "If you are desperate and need God to intervene in your life, come up to the front and let us pray with you." He was speaking to me. I wanted so badly to feel again. Just like that thirteen-year-old at a youth conference in Florida, I rushed to the front and begged for prayer.

Three hours later, I left the church building. I've heard it said that tears heal, and I must have been healed because I cried a lot of them that day. I felt changed. I felt lighter. And I thought back to the time I first committed my life to ministry. The memory seemed both nostalgic and like a proverbial cattle prod poking me in the rear. Once again, I wanted others to know of the beautiful, life-giving, secure, and joyous faith I had received from God. I felt like the lost sheep that had been found. People of faith have altar moments and turning points in their lives, and this was another one on the list for me.

* * *

After I graduated from college in just over three years, I went straight to work at a job I knew would never be permanent. The natural and passionate student in me had wondered for a long time if graduate school was the best next step, but being in your early twenties can be a tricky time if you aren't totally sure what you want to do with your life. I applied to some prestigious theology schools and even got accepted to some, but nothing felt right yet. Part of me now sees that God was humbling my spirit, as He recognized that any degree from a pedigreed school would have been more about me than Him. I continued working and waiting for God to direct my steps.

Then the pastor at my church mentioned a school in California. I'd never heard of it before, which gave me pause. Shouldn't any degree worth having come from a school with a known name? Despite this apprehension, I decided to dip my toe in through an online class. If nothing else, I figured, the experience would give me an intellectual challenge for the time being.

This time of my life was marked by restlessness—a dissatisfaction with the status quo, combined with hope for the future and a competing fear of the unknown. What on earth did God want to do with me? I wasn't quite sure, though I was beginning to understand what it meant to listen for His voice. I waited, prayed, and planned to take my online course. I felt a season of change was coming around the bend, but I wasn't quite sure what it would be.

On a whim, or maybe in response to feeling unsettled, I made a logical move: I went house shopping! I know, I know—not exactly a small step to take for someone who has absolutely no clue what she's supposed to be doing with her life. Even so, I found an adorable little house in Greenville, South Carolina, that was in my price range, then went through the process of purchasing it. As I walked through the steps required to make the deal official, I wondered if this move would be the change that settled my soul.

> What on earth did God want to do with me?

Long story short: it wasn't. Just the opposite, in fact. I was left even more dissatisfied after putting so much energy into the process of finding a new home and choosing a new path. Something was not right, and I felt it in my gut. Yet I knew my life could not stay the same. *What gives?* I kept asking God. *What are You trying to tell me?*

As we approached the closing date, I sat down with my parents and began to weep—something I rarely did with them. Why was I so emotional about something that should be exciting for a young person?

My mother looked at me that day and said, "Tasha, why don't you take the money you were saving for the house, move out to California, and take your classes?"

I looked up at her through my tears, and my stomach turned over. Something about what she said registered, and I knew it right away. The thought of changing course and moving to a place I'd never even visited literally made me sick to my stomach. And yet . . . I could not ignore this idea she'd voiced. It felt much bigger in that moment than buying a house and staying close to home.

> A still, small voice whispered in my ear, *Go for it, Tasha. Take the leap.*

A still, small voice whispered in my ear, *Go for it, Tasha. Take the leap.*

My family and I had this heart-to-heart on a Saturday, and classes were slated to start on Wednesday in Van Nuys (a neighborhood of Los Angeles). The next day, I booked a ticket to California—the place that would change my life forever. "The plane goes both ways," I reckoned. "If this is a huge mistake, I can always come home."

Within forty-eight hours, I was on a plane headed west. Though I couldn't have known it then, God was preparing to use this giant leap of faith in ways I never would have dared to dream.

Go for it, Tasha. Take the leap.

I did, and I didn't look back.

* * *

To this day, moving to Los Angeles stands as the most life-changing decision I ever made—and it happened in a heartbeat. Oftentimes we pray for things to happen, and we wait in misery because they're not happening as quickly as we'd like. These moments of waiting can wreak havoc on a person like me, who loves nothing more than a clear plan with directives. But I'm learning that letting God do His work is about releasing the reins and believing that He will do something amazing with whatever we are willing to give Him. It doesn't come naturally to me, but I'm learning.

Sometimes we have to wait on God. Other times we have to jump at opportunities even though they don't look the way we thought they should look. Today, as I practice listening to God's voice, I can see that my tendency to overthink and overanalyze has held me back at times. Leaving for California was an enormous risk, but I took the step in faith, knowing God would redirect me if need be. As my mom always says, "You can't steer a car that ain't movin'." And with God at the wheel, the only thing we can expect for sure is a wild, incredible ride.

> And with God at the wheel, the only thing we can expect for sure is a wild, incredible ride.

Suppose one of you has a hundred sheep and loses one of them. Doesn't he leave the ninety-nine in the open country and go after the lost sheep until he finds it? And when he finds it, he joyfully puts it on his shoulders and goes home. Then he calls his friends and neighbors together and says, "Rejoice with me; I have found my lost sheep." I tell you that in the same way there will be more rejoicing in heaven over one sinner who repents than over ninety-nine righteous persons who do not need to repent.

—Luke 15:4–7

QUESTIONS TO CONSIDER

1. What is one of the biggest risks you've ever taken? Do you have any regrets? What did you learn from the experience?

2. Describe a moment when you felt like you were treading water. What did it feel like? Do you now know what God was doing with that moment in your life?

3. Have you ever made a decision that you felt to be God-led? What did His prompting sound like to you? What message did He deliver to your heart?

Chapter 8

SEMINARY

When I stepped off the plane in Los Angeles, I didn't know a soul in the city. I didn't have a car, a bed, or even a ride from the airport. The thought, *What on earth have I done?* ran through my head more than a few times as I looked around at my strange new home. Oh, and did I mention that I arrived in the middle of the night? Not an easy way for a twenty-year-old to start her new life!

God's provision found its way to me almost immediately. Someone affiliated with the seminary gave me a ride to the place I was staying, and within a month, someone else had given me furniture and a car. (That's right; I said *given*.) I found a job to cover my bills, and I even found a church home. Through it all, God's peace rested over me like a heavy, warm blanket.

The King's Seminary turned out to be what I hoped it would be: a school that balanced the textbook learning I wanted with the heart knowledge of God that I craved.

My reasons for wanting to attend graduate school had been simple: I wanted to be educated if I was going to minister to people. After my past painful experiences, it was especially important to me

> Through it all, God's peace rested over me like a heavy, warm blanket.

that I become a prepared and well-informed person of faith who took her responsibilities seriously. The last thing I wanted was to repeat the mistakes others had made— mistakes that had done harm to me. If I was going to minister to others, I wanted to be equipped for the task. At seminary, I would learn more about what the Bible really said and how to be an emotionally healthy leader. And I might learn to read some Hebrew along the way.

* * *

Initially during my seminary years, I stayed away from music. The wounds were too deep, and I thought music in any capacity would only bring that pain to the surface.

So when a woman named Kim approached me out of the blue and asked if I'd be interested in leading worship, I balked.

Kim Maas was in charge of the women's ministry at The King's Seminary. "I'm looking for someone to lead worship," she said, "and your name came to mind while I was praying. Do you have any experience doing that? We could really use you, if so!"

No one at the seminary knew I used to sing in church, play guitar, or lead worship. Not Kim or anyone else. That was part of my past—ancient, buried history. And I wanted to keep it that way.

"No, I'm sorry, but I don't do that," I lied.

Kim looked a bit puzzled, but she let it go.

Not for long, though. A week later, she approached me again.

"I know you said you don't lead worship, but every time I pray about it, your name comes to me. Will you at least think on it for a little while? Don't answer yes or no today. Just sit with the idea and talk to God about it."

You may know from experience that it's hard to turn down a godly, determined woman. Church ladies are forces to be reckoned with, and God doesn't hesitate to use them when He wants to get something done. So the next day I called Kim on the phone and fessed up—told her all about my experiences in South Carolina and the reasons I'd abandoned music. I was so nervous and scared to even be talking about music again, but when God forces your hand like that, what else are you supposed to do?

Kim's kind persistence revealed to me that maybe God wasn't done with music in my life. Once again, His voice was coming through, and I was getting better at hearing it. I felt deep in my spirit that this thing I had once loved, that had been lying dormant in my life, might be reemerging on God's terms. Even though I was terrified, I trusted Him to lead me.

The calluses on my fingers had long since worn away, and my voice was nowhere near performance-ready. I knew getting back into singing and playing would be an ugly process, and it was! But my heart told me it was right, and I felt the glory of God in it. The call on my life from so many years before returned to me once again. Only God could have put me back in a place to lead worship, and I had to trust His reasons.

> Only God could have put me back in a place to lead worship, and I had to trust His reasons.

The years I spent in graduate school turned out to be an enormous step in my healing. The program at The

King's Seminary challenged and uplifted me, and I forged some powerful and enduring relationships. Kim is still a close friend of mine, and I have enjoyed watching her traveling the world as an evangelist in more recent years. Yes, she was instrumental in my return to music, but she was also someone who taught me the value of strong female friendships. She brought me into a small group of women who became my core encouragers for the years that followed. For both of those things, I'll forever be grateful.

* * *

In the decades since, I've forgotten so many of the dates and historical facts that were taught in the classroom. But the overarching theme of my seminary education—the lesson I've carried closest to me through the years—was about servant leadership. The King's Seminary taught me at every step that a believer's purpose was—and is—to bring glory to God as we serve one another. That's the entire point, folks. Though my life until then had been about chasing the A or the win, this special time schooled me on the goal of becoming Christlike. And as my career progressed and I encountered forces that challenged this orientation of the heart, the idea of servant leadership was a lesson worth coming back to again and again.

In his letter to the Ephesians, Paul wrote, "I became a servant of this gospel by the gift of God's grace given me through the working of his power" (Ephesians 3:7). Though it's easy to lose sight of what matters most when faced with temptations and trials, serving God is such a privilege and a gift. What an honor it is to know, through God's grace, that you and I have been offered a position on His team—to serve the people He made and loved, and to share with them the love He promises.

Just before graduation, I completed my final course in Israel. Talk about a special and moving place to cross the finish line! We visited numerous holy sites that I had only read about in books, including the Mount of Olives and the famed Western Wall (also known as the Wailing Wall). Because many believe the wall to be a gateway to heaven, it is usually bustling with religious pilgrims who come with their written prayers and slip the slivers of paper into the crevices of the rock.

When our group visited, I wrote a prayer of my own. As I stepped forward, prepared to place my prayer into whatever cracked stone I could find, I was overwhelmed with emotion. I could sense the weight of everyone's fervent prayers, as many around me wept and cried out in various languages for loved ones and desperate situations.

In that moment, I felt the sacredness of the space. Many spiritual pilgrims had come before me, and many would also come after.

As the crowd moved and I stepped forward toward the wall, the only space available was between a very young woman or teenager and another woman who had clearly lived through many decades. The girl was dressed in full army fatigues, and she had a machine gun strapped to her back. This is not uncommon in Israel, as young people join the military quite early. I was simply taken aback by thoughts of how different these two women's lives probably were—and how different my life in the United States was from theirs. I wondered what they were praying for or for whom they were praying. Compassion arose within me as I watched the young girl wipe tears from her face. We were three daughters of God, all distinct in age and history, all in need of God's help, love, and forgiveness.

After I finished my study tour in Jerusalem and the surrounding area, I decided to spend time in Tel Aviv

Many spiritual pilgrims had come before me, and many would also come after.

before coming back to the States. I listened to reggae music, enjoyed Ethiopian food, lay on the beach, and ate my fill of olives. The entire experience left me feeling secure in my faith and firm in my foundation, and I had no regrets about that hurried decision to jump on a red-eye and leave South Carolina behind.

As I prepared to say goodbye to King's, I braced myself for the future unknown. Was I ready for what God had in store?

> *If anyone speaks, they should do so as one who speaks the very words of God. If anyone serves, they should do so with the strength God provides, so that in all things God may be praised through Jesus Christ. To him be the glory and the power for ever and ever.*
>
> —1 Peter 4:11

QUESTIONS TO CONSIDER

1. Describe a time when God surprised you by fully meeting your needs. What did He provide, and how did you respond to His gift?

2. When you study Scripture, what are you looking for? What is something God has revealed to you lately about His Word?

3. Can you think of a moment when God used another person to bring you back to your calling? How comfortable do you feel inviting others to church, Bible study, or other God-centered events?

Chapter 9

THE PLAN

Since I love to make lists, I used to have a five-year plan on paper. (Yes, I can be super type A. You may have observed this about me by now!) I had just graduated from my master's program, was working at a church in Los Angeles, and was doing another administrative job to supplement my income. I was twenty-five years old, and between working and trying to keep my life afloat in an expensive city, I didn't have much of a social life. To say I was too busy and exhausted to enjoy myself would have been a huge understatement. But I still had my priorities straight! (Or so I thought.)

Before long, I realized nothing was going the way I wanted it to—at least, not on my timetable. I would look at that piece of paper and become so frustrated and sad, especially because I thought my list was full of God-given goals and dreams. To be fair, it also included some things that were totally out of my control, such as "Find a husband" and "Marry him." How absurd for me to think I could control this! All the same, I'd look at that list and wonder, *Why are You holding out on me, God? What is wrong here? Did I do something to deserve this?* I'd come so far in my faith journey, yet I couldn't figure it out.

One day I couldn't take it anymore. I was tired and discouraged from working too hard only for nothing to go my way. With a big red marker, I scratched out the entire list. Then I taped it up on my wall. For the longest time, I would look at that list of failed plans every time I walked out the door.

* * *

It was around this same time that I had a truly epic meltdown in my car. Do you ever have those? Something about the solitude of a small, enclosed space seems to make for the perfect "I'm just going to lose it now" spot. In Los Angeles traffic, where the freeways can double as parking lots, I often found myself with loads of time to stew over my thoughts. And on this particular day, I was ripe and ready for a breakdown.

My administrative job was not exactly fulfilling, and though it paid some bills, it felt like a road to nowhere. If you've ever had a job that demanded a lot from you but promised little in return, you get it. To boot, my boss at this job could be a bit difficult. That day, my boss had gotten into an argument with someone in front of me. Not knowing what else to do in that situation, I packed up my things, got in my car, and headed home.

Then someone cut me off in traffic.

And someone flipped me the bird.

And I lost it.

I don't remember pulling the car over, but I managed to find a place to stop the car and experience the ultimate meltdown. Tears poured down my face, and I screamed and screamed. I even remember thinking, *Is this what a breakdown is like? What on earth is happening to me?* For the next three hours, I wailed and prayed and let out emotions that I'd been bottling up for some time. All of my anxieties, disappointments, desperation, fears, and shame came tumbling out in a torrent—almost like I was finally admitting to myself the things God already knew were wrong in my life. My brain was so foggy, I also don't remember driving home, eating dinner, or going to bed. I felt like part of me died that afternoon, and I was operating as half a person.

It's funny how something as mundane as a bad day at work or in traffic can crack you wide open. After my epic meltdown, I spent a few days grieving and coming to grips with the feelings I'd finally voiced. I knew in my heart of hearts that none of this was a mystery to God; He knew—and knows—me better than I know myself. But it's not an easy thing to reckon with feelings you've tried so hard to push down. In a way, part of me really *had* died:

> It was one small thought, but in that instant, my life started to blossom.

the version of myself I thought I *should* be. That Tasha needed to disappear before the more authentic version of myself could step into her place and claim the plans God had for her.

A short time later, I was staring at that marred red list once again. It still hung on the wall, a haunting list of failures. The words represented so much of my disappointment and loneliness, yet my heart had already begun to shift. Were any of those plans right for me to begin with? I took a deep breath and let these words flow through me:

Not my plans. Not my will. But Yours be done, Lord.

I opened up my hands. It was one small thought, but in that instant, my life started to blossom.

* * *

Relying on God has never been the easiest thing for me. Time and time again, He has proven Himself worthy of my trust, but my flesh is weak in this regard. When I try to control things beyond my grasp or make plans without God's input, it's usually because I'm not trusting Him to handle the matters of my life. Trying to control everything on my own is a defense mechanism of sorts—an effort rooted in doubt. When I fail to believe that God is working for my good and on my behalf, I make a desperate grab for those reins. Then when my misguided plans fail spectacularly, the whole cycle starts again.

A man with a possessed son in the New Testament is famous for saying to Jesus, "I do believe; help me overcome my unbelief!" (Mark 9:24). This is one of the lessons God may spend my life teaching me: that He is worthy of trust, that I do not have to earn His love, and that He has good plans for my life. Fortunately, He is patient. And

I am willing to try again. He has already taught me so much, and I know there is a marked difference in me as a result of His never-ending, gentle direction.

I don't live in Los Angeles anymore, but I still get to visit from time to time. One of the first things you notice about the city when you get there is the palm trees that line the old streets. They are so tall and slender—truly striking and beautiful. But they are also incredibly strong. One might think a tree that thin would snap like a twig in a windstorm, but the palm trees of LA are no strangers to the Santa Ana winds. Whenever the downslope winds howl through the city, palm fronds and pieces of tree trunk litter the roads and wreak havoc. But the trees themselves stand tall.

Like most old trees, the palms have learned resistance. Time and exposure to powerful winds have made them strong and flexible, not weak and flimsy. As they've been hardened to the elements, their roots have also grown deeper and deeper into the ground. The result is a deceptively sturdy object—a living creature that can survive almost anything. Yes, when the winds come, the palms may lose some of their fronds. But those fronds probably needed to be pruned off anyway. They will grow stronger without the extra weight.

I want the stamina of those palm trees. No, I don't look forward to the wind, but I know it will inevitably come. Not one of us can escape every grief, unexpected diagnosis, abuse, betrayal, or loss—the things that can either destroy our faith or cause us to lean into it. In 2 Corinthians 11, the apostle Paul described being imprisoned, hungry, shipwrecked, flogged, and more—all so he could "boast of the things that show [his] weakness" (verse 30).

Though I may fight against God's will at times, may He use each of my weaknesses to help me better trust Him and understand His goodness. In the moments when I remember and accept that God is good, that He wants good things for me, and that I can't do anything to make Him love me less, everything begins to change again.

> Though I may fight against God's will at times, may He use each of my weaknesses to help me better trust Him and understand His goodness.

Blessed is the one who trusts in the LORD,
whose confidence is in him.
They will be like a tree planted by the water
that sends out its roots by the stream.
It does not fear when heat comes;
its leaves are always green.
It has no worries in a year of drought
and never fails to bear fruit.
—Jeremiah 17:7–8

QUESTIONS TO CONSIDER

1. Try to think of a time when your plans didn't line up with God's. How did you react? What did you learn from the experience?

2. How has a struggle in your life made you stronger? Can you think of a weakness that God has used for your strength?

3. What does it look like to trust God with everything? Is letting go of the reins easy for you?

Chapter 10

AMERICAN IDOL

As I began releasing my plans to God, some exciting and unexpected things began to happen. I was still working in ministry at my church, which provided a real sense of purpose as well as a fun circle of friends. I was in my midtwenties, and the show *American Idol* was still popular at the time. My friends from church and I would often get together to watch the show, then we'd chatter about the contestants and the results before and after services. It was our watercooler conversation, but that's as far as it went for me.

Friends and family who knew I could sing had suggested I try out for years. Per usual, I had my doubts. First, I didn't think trying out would get me anywhere. Second, I wondered if the music industry ever truly respected those who gained their success from reality television. But when a cattle call audition was scheduled for the Rose Bowl, several more people urged me to give it a shot. Some friends and I decided that it would be fun to go together, so the night before, we said, "Why not?" If nothing else, we'd have a good time hanging out and collect some great stories to tell later.

When we arrived at the Rose Bowl the next morning, we got in line with around fourteen thousand other people. Some had camped out all night, and others set up grills for cookouts in the line. It was a fun experience to be there with so many excited people who all loved the show and had dreams to pursue. As we waited there together, a secret hope of my own welled up within me—not necessarily that I'd go far with the audition, but rather that a door would open up inside me as I stepped out into this experience. Maybe trying something new would spur some much-needed changes for me, I hoped. That was pretty much all I wanted.

Much to my dismay, I made it to the next stage of the process after auditioning for the show's producers. Though TV magic makes it seem like these cattle call auditions all take place within a day or two, it wasn't until months later that I entered the audition room to sing for Randy, Simon, Kara DioGuardi, and a wide-eyed guest judge named Katy Perry. Feeling like I had nothing to lose, I sang "Baby Baby Baby" by Joss Stone and got a unanimous "yes" vote to move on to Hollywood Week. Fortunately for me, Hollywood was in my backyard, but I was still stunned to be one of three hundred chosen to move on from the cattle calls. I didn't know what to make of any of it!

Hollywood Week was overwhelming for obvious reasons, primarily because I didn't know so many of the songs we were supposed to sing. I had grown up listening mostly to Christian music—not exactly what *American Idol* is known for! I had to stay up late every night trying to memorize lyrics and melodies, which exhausted me and made me feel like I was behind everyone else.

My learning curve was steep, and every round of cuts tested my confidence, but I rose to the occasion and treated every opportunity like a treasure. By the end of the week, I had learned so much and met some of the amazing other contestants, including Lauren Daigle, Tori Kelly, Luke Edgemon, Todrick Hall, and Sharon Wilbur.

Hollywood Week came to a close, and I was cut from the top sixty contestants. Though rejection never feels great, a wave of relief rushed over me as I left the hotel and headed home. Deep down I had never really thought I would win *Idol*, but the experience had revealed a lot to me and forced me to ask some questions I'd never really faced. I'd wrestled with my own insecurities while also considering what it meant to be a public-facing person, and I'm not sure any other experience could have opened my heart up the way auditioning for *American Idol* did.

Despite being mentally wrung out, the week left me feeling energized. Something about it all had felt so right, and I now had to examine that feeling. To that point, my singing experience had been about worshiping God in ministry—not about singing for myself or others. A huge part of being a worship leader is getting out of the way, but singing in the secular world is all about performing and being noticed for it. I couldn't reconcile in my head why performing felt so easy and natural despite my past experience.

> I couldn't reconcile in my head why performing felt so easy and natural despite my past experience.

Getting cut from the show when I did freed me up to consider new paths for myself—paths I'd never even imagined before. Soon after, I met with my pastor and confessed my confusing feelings about the experience. "So *Idol* made me really think," I told him. "I think I might be called to do music in some ways that take me outside of what I'm doing here at the church."

He looked at me and nearly cracked up. "Tasha, we've all known that for years," he said. "We've just been waiting for *you* to figure it out!"

How could I ignore a blessing like that? I was so grateful for the supportive church family I'd had for so long—people who had helped me heal from my teenage years of singing. So I began to talk to God about it. I prayed, *God, whatever they may be, I want my next steps to be about You. Open the right doors for me in Your time.* I'd gone against His will enough times to know that I would only find peace if I followed Him.

* * *

Not long after that conversation with my pastor, I was asked to help lead worship for a multilevel marketing conference in Orange County. (Listen: I know it's random. But sometimes God does random stuff, OK?) You never know who you're going to meet at a place like that, and on this day, I met Kesha's keyboardist. She told me they were looking for a background singer—someone both Kesha and Rihanna could share on their Japanese tour. That's right: Kesha *and* Rihanna. Both superstars. In *Japan*. I had asked God to open a door, but it seemed He had opened a floodgate.

She asked if I would be interested in auditioning. But before I answered her, I went to the bathroom to have a moment. I said a little prayer and asked for God's direction. When I felt some peace, I came back to her and said, "Yes, I'd love to audition. Here's my number." In almost no time at all, the tour's musical director called me. I auditioned and got the job—simple as that. Talk about a whirlwind!

Don't do it, Tasha.
Don't go. This isn't it.

I was supposed to start rehearsing on a Wednesday afternoon. But that same morning, I felt this tiny feeling: *Don't do it, Tasha. Don't go. This isn't it.*

I didn't understand what I was hearing. God had made this part almost easy for me, and I had sensed the forthcoming shift in my life. Why would God open this door, only to tell me to close it? I had a decision to make—and fast. Some of my friends thought I was self-sabotaging, but I knew what I needed to do. I called up the musical director and backed out three hours before my start time.

This could have been a really reckless move, and after I got off the phone, I panicked. Had I just thrown away my shot? And for what—a feeling? A voice? The music business could be a small world, and to abandon ship at such a late hour could have ruined my name among the people with the power to hire and fire. But I had vowed to listen for God each step of the way, and His message had been clear: *Don't do it, Tasha.*

I had almost instant regret. This job would have been the kind of opportunity most singers would kill for, and some people live in LA for decades hoping for the kind of break I'd just forfeited. I had no clout, little professional experience, and no guarantee of ever getting a chance like this again. Not to mention, it would have solved most of my money problems. Los Angeles was not exactly a cost-effective place to live, after all. What in the world had I just done?

> God had shown up—again. And He was doing something more significant than ever before.

That same day, during the very hour I should have reported to my first rehearsal, I got a phone call that changed my life. God had shown up—again. And He was doing something more significant than ever before.

The LORD said, "Go out and stand on the mountain in the presence of the LORD, for the LORD is about to pass by." Then a great and powerful wind tore the mountains apart and shattered the rocks before the LORD, but the LORD was not in the wind. After the wind there was an earthquake, but the LORD was not in the earthquake. After the earthquake came a fire, but the LORD was not in the fire. And after the fire came a gentle whisper.
—1 Kings 19:11–12

QUESTIONS TO CONSIDER

1. Describe a moment in your life when God showed up and surprised you. Did He open a door you weren't expecting? Did He shut a door you were expecting to be opened? What did you take away from the experience?

2. What is something that could have been perceived as a failure but has turned out to be a success in your life?

3. Have you ever turned down an opportunity, only to soon be presented with a better one? If so, did you see God behind it?

Chapter 11

SALT

"Can you be here in twenty minutes, Tasha?"

I was stunned by the question. It was two o'clock in the afternoon, and I was still reeling from my last-minute decision to turn down the job touring with Kesha and Rihanna. The person on the other end of the line was a manager calling from Katy Perry's team. Yes, *that* Katy Perry. Turned out they needed a background singer too. I didn't even know how they'd gotten my number.

My mind reeled. How was all of this happening in the span of one day? "Uhh, yes, I can," I stammered. "I'll do my best." I spoke before I could even think.

Could I actually get to this audition in time? Los Angeles could be such a bottleneck, but I had already cleared the day's schedule for the job I'd just turned down.

If I was going to make it to the studio, I couldn't waste another moment.

God, what is happening? What am I doing? What are You doing?

I headed to my car and downloaded a few songs onto my phone, including "California Gurls," her latest single. As I raced across town, I tried my hardest to practice some of Katy's music and get my head in the game. The stress of the morning, my instant regret, and now this unexpected development had turned my brain to mush—but I was full of energy and hope. My whole body was a live wire.

I parked my car and walked into SIR Studios in Hollywood. Fortunately, the only other high-stakes audition I'd done had prepared me for what this one would be like. I introduced myself, sang a tune with Katy's band, then met Katy (again) for a short conversation. The whole audition happened so fast that I didn't even have enough time to get nervous!

The next day, I was officially hired and began rehearsals. And this time, all signs pointed to *yes*. Everything about this opportunity seemed so much better than the one I'd turned down. I could only imagine that God—for reasons not yet known to me—had rerouted me to this place with these people. Two days later, I was on the road with the

Katy Perry tour. First stop: a smallish, humble venue in New York City known as Madison Square Garden. It was the first stop of a four-year journey—one full of international destinations, private planes, celebrity meetups, award shows, and many other surreal experiences. It was also an intense time of growth and learning, as I worked out with God what it meant to be a Christian in a setting unlike any other I'd known before.

I could only imagine that God—for reasons not yet known to me—had rerouted me to this place with these people.

* * *

Auditioning for *American Idol* may not have led to a big win on a reality TV show, but it had opened my heart and mind. I'd finally felt free to express myself in new, creative ways, and with God's help, I hoped to navigate this new lane in a way that continued to bring glory to Him. To some, a career shift into the music industry could have seemed like a major shock. And to someone on the outside looking in, it could seem like my life was switching directions entirely. To me, it felt very natural—like I had been meant to do it all along. The ease of the transition made me wonder why it had taken me so long to start making decisions I knew were right for me instead of doing what I thought I *should* do. Was I living for God, or was I operating out of a fear of people and how they would react?

After I accepted the job with Katy, some people had a lot of opinions about it. I had already begun wrestling with the shift in my career, but to others, it was a blatantly bad choice. They wondered how on earth a worship leader could be called to go on a secular music tour, and they reached out to express as much. I had no response except to say that I felt the grace to do it. God had paved a way for me, and I had listened to His directives in obedience. Sure, people were judging me, but a big lesson I've learned in this business is to listen to God and God alone. Not every opinion is for your good, and not every loud voice is worth heeding. Back then, I was still learning

> God had paved a way for me, and I had listened to His directives in obedience.

that lesson—so those frustrated phone calls were not easy for me.

One thing I've always known is that salt can't season anything inside the saltshaker. The salt's gotta come out somehow. We can silo ourselves within the four walls of a church building, or we can go with God out into the world and be lights for Him. While I didn't think of my job as a giant evangelism opportunity, I did hope to represent God well. And if God wanted specific things from me during that time, my heart was open to His direction.

* * *

If you're still wondering how Katy Perry's team ever found me in the first place, here's your answer. (It took me a while to figure it out too.) Right after *Idol*, I had gone to a friend's dinner party and met a handful of people. A mutual friend introduced me to someone who— unbeknownst to me—was Katy's tour manager. Our exchange was probably thirty seconds long, but when Katy was in a crunch, this man remembered my name, remembered seeing me on *Idol*, and suggested someone reach out. Katy herself didn't remember me from *Idol* at all—my hair had changed a bit in the interim—but this man did. He'd tossed my hat into the ring after speaking to me for under a minute. The rest, as they say, is history.

Months into the tour, we were in Europe doing a performance for *Germany's Next Topmodel*. I was touching up my makeup when Katy ran into my dressing room and took me by the shoulders. "You were on *Idol*!" she said. "I was your guest judge!"

I cracked up at her realization. "Yeah, Katy. You're just now figuring this out?" We both had a good laugh about it.

You are the light of the world. A town built on a hill cannot be hidden. Neither do people light a lamp and put it under a bowl. Instead they put it on its stand, and it gives light to everyone in the house. In the same way, let your light shine before others, that they may see your good deeds and glorify your Father in heaven.
—Matthew 5:14–16

QUESTIONS TO CONSIDER

1. Describe a moment when someone had a problem with a decision you made. How did you respond to their criticism? Did you allow your fear of humans to surpass your fear of God?

2. What does it mean to be salt leaving the saltshaker? As we represent God in untraditional spaces, how should we go about it?

3. How have events you didn't understand in the moment prepared you for other things that came later in your life?

Chapter 12

ON THE ROAD

Going on tour with seventy-five strangers was unlike anything I'd ever done. First of all, I'd never been part of such a massive operation! Going from the pulpit to the pop stage was an adjustment, to say the least. Second, I was one of only a couple people who classified themselves as Christian on the tour, which was obviously *quite* different from working for a church. But those new circumstances taught me how to love without judgment, and I never felt the need to try to change anyone. Before this major season change, I think I had underestimated the power of God inside of me. Jesus Himself said to His followers, "Your love for one another will prove to the world that you are my disciples" (John 13:35 NLT). I was called to love them. People knew what I believed, and they respected it.

As you can imagine, touring full-time meant upending my entire life. When I said yes to this job, I said goodbye to my apartment, my car, my routine, and my normalcy. Suddenly I was traveling the world and living out of a suitcase, losing track of the time zone. The lifestyle was disorienting at times, and I was so grateful for family and friends back home who stayed in touch despite being half a world away. When you're on the move like that, you naturally detach from some things—and I had to fight for my grip on the relationships that mattered.

> People knew what I believed, and they respected it.

Most of the time I just looked around at what was happening and thought, *Is this really my life right now?* In the early days of the tour, we performed "California Gurls" with Snoop Dogg at the MTV Video Music Awards, and as I was getting my hair and makeup done, Betty White appeared backstage. That's right: *the* Betty White. She sat next to me getting her hair and makeup done, and I was almost too nervous to speak to her! Moments later I was onstage, singing in sunglasses and bopping along while Katy wore a blue wig and levitated through the air on a surfboard. All in a day's work!

To sum up those years in a few paragraphs would be impossible because I could fill a book up with all the crazy things I got to do. We played the GRAMMYs, we played for American troops, we performed on *Saturday Night Live* and *Late Show with David Letterman*, and so much more. I flew on private planes and stayed in five-star hotels in countries all over the world. I performed for powerful politicians, built a massive collection of wigs, and met artists from Stevie Wonder to Miley Cyrus. I realize that none of these are normal situations *at all.*

Katy herself was such a bright light. She was so street-smart, and she was strong but managed to stay softhearted. When our team would cross paths with other tour groups, it became abundantly clear that our work atmosphere was so much healthier and more positive than many others. I attribute a lot of that to Katy, who

> I learned a lot about the importance of surrounding yourself with good, trustworthy people.

was careful about who she hired. Just by watching her and observing our team, I learned a lot about the importance of surrounding yourself with good, trustworthy people. And when you're in close quarters with people for months and months, you figure out pretty quickly who they *really* are.

Though we could've easily grown sick of each other, I even found myself calling people from the tour on our off days. I'd pick up the phone and say, "Hey, do you wanna get coffee?" to someone I'd just spent a hundred straight days with. The friendships were real and still are. All these years later, we touch base regularly and stay in the loop on important developments in each other's lives. I'm not sure if that's typical for coworkers who basically lived together, but we established genuine bonds. We visited Turkish baths, got piranha pedicures, and ate food we couldn't identify. Those experiences and people will stick with me always.

Katy was also extremely generous with us. She'd take us on vacations and other excursions on our days off, such as a water park or a movie theater she'd rented out for us. It was a luxury for us to enjoy a film together without being interrupted. ATVs in Dubai, spelunking in New Zealand. . . . Without really trying, I filled my passport with stamps, and now it reads like a novel. Not a day goes by that I don't thank God for the incredible things I've been able to see and do. My bucket list has been whittled down to just a handful of items after seeing so much of this wide world. To say I feel blessed would be the under-statement of the century.

* * *

At one point, Katy called me to tell me she was letting me go from the tour. I understood her reasons; they weren't personal, she said. Her music was simply going in a different direction, and she was looking for a different sound. I respected so much that she was willing to break the news herself rather than rely on some lackey to do the dirty work. It was as amicable a work breakup as I could've imagined.

Weeks later, she called me back. They had auditioned several singers and even hired some replacements, but they weren't quite working out. "I'm so sorry," she told me. "Please forgive me. Sometimes you don't know what you have until you lose it." She asked to hire me back but with a raise.

Some people would let pride get in the way of a call like that, but not Katy. Sure, it was a bit weird being fired and rehired, but I went with it. I listened to some of our older performances to see how or if I could adjust my sound this time around. But coming back was not all that difficult because the bridges had never been burned. By then, Katy was one of the most famous people on the planet, and she could've gotten away with almost any behavior she chose; instead, she operated with professional humility and grace.

* * *

These days I still hit the road to sing, but it looks pretty different. It's a lot of "weekend warrior" traveling, which is much better for my family and me. I hope that when my kids, Levi and Lyla, are older, they will have fond memories of the shows Keith and I took them to, but I also hope they will grow up feeling like they had a steady and happy childhood. We work hard to keep things as even-keeled as possible for the kids, and I'm grateful for our cozy home base.

I also think back on my time with Katy and how it prepared me for the life I'm living now. Though I knew she was incredibly street-smart, I don't think I fully appreciated the burden that was on her shoulders. So many jobs depended on her, and it must have been hard for her to know who to trust. When you're as famous as Katy Perry, you can attract the worst types of people—and it must have been tiring to wonder if the ones close to her were of the trustworthy or manipulative sort. While some might assume that fame is all about outrageous living and stacks of cash, it can take an enormous toll on the person experiencing it.

Katy held her cards close to the vest because she had to. Her career—and to an extent, our livelihoods—depended on it. That's a weight she carried that I understand much more now. It's a shock to wake up one day and discover that your voice and decisions have influence, but I don't think Katy ever took those responsibilities lightly. She struck me as a person who was careful with her words and decisions, and I'm grateful I was around to learn from that example.

> While some might assume that fame is all about outrageous living and stacks of cash, it can take an enormous toll on the person experiencing it.

As my career continues to grow, I treasure these memories and lessons. My time on tour seems to have laid the groundwork for what was to come: a wholly different kind of music career. My perspective on the spotlight, though, is atypical because I've already seen enough to know fame is not worth craving. "Success" as the world defines it is not always what it's cracked up to be, and I consider myself fortunate to have come to that knowledge during my years in the music industry in Los Angeles. Call it what you will, but that preparation feels like God's protection.

In your hearts revere Christ as Lord. Always be prepared to give an answer to everyone who asks you to give the reason for the hope that you have. But do this with gentleness and respect, keeping a clear conscience.
—1 Peter 3:15–16

QUESTIONS TO CONSIDER

1. What words would you use to describe God? Try to use scriptures to back up your answer.
2. What responsibilities do people of influence have when it comes to others? What have you learned from people you considered to be generous and gifted leaders?
3. Describe a time when someone apologized to you sincerely. How did it make you feel, and what did the apology do for your relationship?

Chapter 13

AFRICA

Though I would travel with Katy's tour for four or five months at a time, I tried to stay connected to my home church in Los Angeles. Part of that meant regularly touching base with my core ladies' group, and another part involved doing missions work on my time off. For one of those trips, I met up with a team from my church in Kenya. Since I was a little girl, I had wanted to travel to Africa—so when a friend mentioned a trip she was planning, I told her I was going with her. She didn't even ask me; I just invited myself!

I could not have been more excited for this trip. To prepare, I did my research on our destinations, watched documentaries, and even tried to learn a little Swahili. Sometimes I am completely spontaneous and unprepared, and other times the planning and overachieving side of me takes over. But I also knew that I couldn't fully prepare for the experience to come.

From the first moment, Nairobi was an adventure. For many Westerners, traveling in Africa can be, well . . . challenging. Africans' sense of time tends to be much different from Americans' sense, for example. A simple task of transporting people and luggage from one place to another can prove to take a very long time. Emphasis on *very*. But one thing I've learned from traveling is that if you lean into the culture you're visiting, you will learn to love what it brings to your soul. Just because we're used to one way of life doesn't mean it's the best way.

> Just because we're used to one way of life doesn't mean it's the best way.

The Africans I developed relationships with were more concerned with relationship than agenda. Everyone moved together and took time to take care of one another. Everyone's happiness or contentment seemed to be based more on the community's health than the individual's. What I experienced was a warm and caring group of people, and I was grateful to learn from them.

We spent part of our trip traveling to remote villages, which was a challenge all its own. On one such trip to the

Masai Mara region, we were driving late into the night and encountering washed-out roads. It was the rainy season, and our only option was to physically push our vans out of the rivers that had formed across the road.

We got stuck a couple of times, but the men in our group were able to push us forward. At one particular impasse, though, we knew it was going to be difficult. We didn't have any choice but to try; we couldn't turn back. It was already so late and dark, and there was nowhere to go.

My stomach was sick with nerves. I just knew we weren't going to make it across the river. Large rocks had washed into our path, and water rushed all around the van. Plus, we were in the middle of reserve land—meaning animals, not to mention mosquitoes, all around us!

Prayer seemed like our only option. I could feel the discouraging situation weighing heavily on everyone. I prayed, *God, please shine Your light on us right now . . . show us the way forward.*

Just then, I remembered something I had packed. For Christmas the year before, my parents had given me a high-powered LED bike lamp for night riding on trails. When I say high-powered, I mean it could light up an entire backyard and blind someone if they looked straight at it. I wondered if the thing was even legal! Though I am an extremely light packer and do *not* like bringing things

I will not need, something in my gut had told me to bring this bike lamp. I scrambled through my luggage to find it and offered it to the men trying to move the bus.

The light was bright enough to illuminate the entire area where we were stuck. With the light pouring over everything, we could better see our problem and better understand it for what it was. That'll preach, won't it? Sometimes you just need a little of God's light over a situation.

> Sometimes you just need a little of God's light over a situation.

I'm not sure if it was our prayers or the giant light shining from the river, but some strong Masai men appeared and came to our rescue. They're considered some of the tallest people in the world and are known for being strong, so, they were helpful. For the next few hours, that crazy-strong bike light assisted the men who worked together to shove us out of the river and back onto a drivable road. Meanwhile the battery on that lamp lasted for what felt like a miraculous amount of time. Later on during that trip, I got a life-changing message.

* * *

Weeks before, on the previous leg of Katy's tour, we had performed at the opening of the Cricket World Cup in Chennai, India. While there, I thought to myself that I should take advantage of the moment and spend some time backpacking around the country. It was the kind of place I might not ever visit again on my own dime, so I set off on a solo adventure.

I was flying out of an airport in a smallish city (I can't remember which one), and in the waiting area, I sat in the only seat available. As I got settled, I noticed the man next to me and just had this feeling about him. *This is someone I should know,* I thought. *I am not sure why, but I need to know him.* So we started chatting.

He worked in sports and Christian radio, he told me, and he had come to India to cover the cricket competition where we'd just performed. But he also was a pastor from Cape Town, South Africa. "You should come lead worship at the church we're starting," he told me. "We could really use your help."

I barely knew this man, but I had this strange sense of peace as we spoke. Our chance encounter seemed unlikely enough. What were the odds that I'd sit next to someone like this in the middle of an Indian airport? Just in case, we exchanged information, then went our separate ways.

When he did reach out via email, I was already in Kenya. My phone rarely had enough signal to check email, but on this day, it did. I opened up his message, which said, "Hey, we're getting started in Cape Town. Are you ready?"

I had another one of those "why not?" moments, so I told him I would come. I was already in Africa anyway, so I changed my ticket and flew to South Africa at the end of my trip. I flew through Johannesburg to Cape Town, and while on the way, my brain caught up with me. I thought, *I don't even really know these people! What the heck am I doing?* The risk was real, but I felt peace about it.

When I landed, he and his family picked me up from the airport. (Spoiler alert: they were nice and normal and *not* criminals at all!) I met the entire church team, they took me into their homes, and they showed me all around the city. They even taught me how to make biltong, the South African version of beef jerky. It was such a cool experience, and to top it all off, I got to lead worship again. That was something I had sorely missed doing.

By this time, my heart had really begun to shift. Deep down, I felt that it was almost time to move on from touring with Katy and the crew. Though I hadn't made the call quite yet, my mind was softening to the idea, and as I looked around at South Africa, I could almost imagine it as a new home. A Christian radio station in town was hiring, and I even looked at buying a house. The opportunities seemed endless there, and the connection I felt with those people was so deep that I could envision an entirely different future for myself. It reminded me of so many other moments in my life when I'd felt God prompting me toward some kind of change.

Ultimately, I decided not to stay. It became clear to me that if I bought a house in South Africa, I might never go home! I really missed my family, so that longing for them won out. At the end of my stay, I said goodbye to the wonderful people I'd met and wished them all the best. I packed up and flew to Malaysia, where I rejoined Katy and the tour after being away for a month.

* * *

When I left Africa and returned to work in Malaysia, the contrast between the two worlds couldn't have been more stark. I'd gone straight from visiting orphanages in Kenya, staying in the bush with the Masai tribe, and witnessing the political unrest of Cape Town, to visiting a gigantic mall in Malaysia. Yes, I'd traveled to the other side of the world, but it felt like another planet altogether. Though I sincerely loved this job and had no regrets about it, I knew deep within that it was time to change gears after all.

As I contemplated the changes to come, I thought back to one of the most extraordinary nights I'd spent outside of Nairobi. The women of a local church had pulled me aside and encircled me. I wasn't sure what was happening, but I felt the seriousness of the moment. As I stood there and waited, they began to sing. Their song made me weep, as had been my response the entire trip whenever someone's gorgeous voice rang out. Music has always made me emotional, but these women sang as if they could move heaven and earth.

> Music has always made me emotional, but these women sang as if they could move heaven and earth.

Two of the women moved closer and began to wrap a large piece of beautiful fabric around my waist. Their movements were methodical, and several of the women joined me in the tear-fest. A few spoke English and began to explain to me what was taking place.

When Kenyan women—all mothers—perform this ritual, they are acknowledging a woman who has become a mother. It is a special tradition reserved for that rite of passage. The women of the church knew I didn't have children and that I wasn't even married. But as they continued singing in Swahili, they told me they were acknowledging me as "a mother of Kenya." I mean, as if I *could* get any more emotional, they had to go and squeeze my heart like that?

What was so stunning about this event for me was that it tapped into one of my deepest desires: to be a mother. It pointed to a time and acknowledged an identity I had not stepped into yet. How was I to know if I would ever get married or have children of my own? I welcomed the Kenyan women's gesture as a reminder from God that He knew my desires and would fulfill them one way or another. It would be years before I would understand what He was doing, but He was doing it all the same.

Then Jesus came to them and said, "All authority in heaven and on earth has been given to me. Therefore go and make disciples of all nations, baptizing them in the name of the Father and of the Son and of the Holy Spirit, and teaching them to obey everything I have commanded you. And surely I am with you always, to the very end of the age."
—Matthew 28:18–20

QUESTIONS TO CONSIDER

1. Describe a moment when God used something of yours (for example: a talent, an experience, a bike light) in a way you never would have expected.
2. What are some lessons you have learned from your brothers and sisters in Christ?
3. What happens in our hearts when we worship God? What is the purpose of gathering together and praising Him?

Chapter 14

SABBATICAL

I got stuck again.

It was different this time, thank goodness. I wasn't suicidal, and I hadn't abandoned my faith. My time with Katy's tour had come to a close, which promised no small adjustment, and when I returned to Los Angeles, things weren't the way I'd left them. For the last several years, I'd traveled from one corner of the planet to another and back again, working hard to keep some part of me tethered to my friends and family. While I succeeded to an extent, I also knew that people had just stopped inviting me to things because for so long I'd only been able to say no. I was not resentful of this, because I knew some relationships just naturally went that way. But it didn't make me feel particularly grounded in Los Angeles anymore.

Then there was the broken engagement. I had dated and gotten engaged to a wonderful guy, but for all kinds of reasons, it didn't pan out. I had picked out a dress . . . we had gone to premarital counseling . . . we had set a date . . . all the things. After we called it off, I was despairing. I was thirty and exhausted by another serious relationship that hadn't ended in a marriage. In the immediate aftermath, I couldn't imagine putting that much effort into anyone else any time soon.

In a larger sense, I was feeling a familiar tension—the internal, soul-deep sensation I've felt when I know the season of my life is changing. This period of time reminded me of the months I had spent working in Los Angeles after seminary and before *American Idol*. I had a job to make ends meet, but I seemed to be swimming in circles. Because I tend to get hung up on the whys of things, I get really frustrated when something I'm doing doesn't seem to have a purpose. And though I was confident that it was time to leave Katy's tour, I was *not* confident of what should come next. The whys and the what-ifs really weighed me down.

I missed South Carolina, and I missed my family. My great aunt was sick, and my grandmother, who deserved credit for much of my spirituality, was also declining. Resorting to my academic and theological jargon, I declared that it was time for me to go home and take a sabbatical. While earlier in life I would've seen a move like that more as defeat, this time I knew I was doing the right thing. I didn't know what I was going to do next; I didn't have a job, and except for family, I wasn't connected to many folks in my hometown. Yet I knew in my heart that I would find some rest and resolve there.

My dad flew out to LA and helped me pack everything I owned into some PODS. Then we began our three-day trek back across the country together. Fortunately, I had plenty of money in the bank, so I decided to take an indefinite break. I didn't know how long it was going to be or what I would do with myself afterward, but it didn't matter. I needed to take one step at a time.

> The goal of my sabbatical was simple: I wanted to be whole.

The goal of my sabbatical was simple: I wanted to be whole. See, you can love your job, travel the world, have the coolest opportunities, make great money, have influence, and still not feel complete. I had friends but didn't know why I still felt lonely. I had a solid career but had lost my sense of purpose. Something was missing, and I needed to figure out what it was. So I ordered every book

I could find about Sabbath rest and holed up with my parents in South Carolina. If I was going to take a sabbatical, I was going to make it the best sabbatical ever taken. I sat on the porch swing every day with a glass of sweet tea or coffee, researching my subject.

When they hear the word *Sabbath*, most people think of the Ten Commandments: "Remember the Sabbath day by keeping it holy. Six days you shall labor and do all your work, but the seventh day is a sabbath to the LORD your God" (Exodus 20:8–10). But let's not forget that God set the ultimate example of Sabbath by resting on the seventh day "from all his work" (Genesis 2:2). Together, the verses reflect a Sabbath's unique importance: God wants rest for us and exemplifies its importance by taking rest for Himself!

Something special about the commandment to rest is that God seemed to know we would need help keeping it. His explanation of it is more elaborate than the other commandments; in the verses devoted to it, we're not only told *what* to do but also *why*. Sabbath applied to men, women, servants, cattle, and even land. It was intended to be a built-in pressure release to save us from ourselves.

Sabbath reminded God's people of who they were and who God was (and is!). If His chosen people could maintain a spirit of remembrance concerning how God had delivered them from Egypt, provided manna in the desert, and been a cloud by day and a fire by night, then they would remember His faithfulness to them.

I had not exactly lost my understanding of God, but I was feeling pretty numb. I craved direction and closeness with Him. As I took the time I needed to rest, pray, and listen for God's prompting, I spent a lot of time alone. And if you've ever had the chance to be alone with your thoughts for a while, you know that solitude can release memories. During those hours of sitting on the back porch in my South Carolina hometown, some old, unresolved emotions came swirling back. Soon, I decided I needed help processing everything that was surfacing. The sabbatical was working in the rest department, but I needed something deeper, something more.

> I had not exactly lost my understanding of God, but I was feeling pretty numb.

And [God] said, "My presence will go with you, and I will give you rest." And [Moses] said to him, "If your presence will not go with me, do not bring us up from here."
—Exodus 33:14–15 ESV

QUESTIONS TO CONSIDER

1. What habits or practices do you have that involve making quiet time for God? If you don't have any, what could you try today that would make space for His presence?

2. What are the many benefits of rest? Why do you think we tend to sacrifice it in our daily lives?

3. Describe something God has revealed to you in a quiet moment. Would you have been able to hear Him without the quiet surrounding you?

Chapter 15

COLORADO

I've been through a lot of counseling. I've been not only for myself, but also for couples counseling, and I've even gone to sessions with other people and offered counseling through my role at the church. On my own time, I've read a plethora of books on counseling and have studied a tremendous amount of psychology, just trying to figure out the human mind. Self-help used to be the only type of book I ever read! This doesn't make me a qualified expert, of course, but I say all of that to explain that when the rubber met the road, self-help and psychology didn't fix me. At the end of the day, I would close the book I'd finished and feel even more frustrated because I knew what I *should* be thinking about a subject, but my reality still felt different. I understood why I was going through something and why I was feeling what I was feeling, but I felt powerless to change any of it.

I'm not discrediting counseling. I think it's one of the best things you can do—for yourself, your marriage, your kids, or almost any relationship. But during my sabbatical, I realized I was just ready to go deeper. I had plenty of tools for understanding what I was going through, but I still needed *healing*. I'd read enough books on the subject and now felt God prompting me toward something more.

> I understood why I was going through something and why I was feeling what I was feeling, but I felt powerless to change any of it.

Several people had recommended an intensive therapy program in Buena Vista, Colorado. The counseling center was called Crossroads, and I decided to spend two weeks there. I had no idea what to expect, but I had heard it was a unique type of faith-based counseling. Enough people had put their stamp of approval on the program to make me feel good about the trip, but deep down I was terrified it wouldn't work. What on earth would I do if this place couldn't help me—or if God wouldn't meet me there? I'd tried everything else, and this felt like a last resort. I arrived ready to do whatever it took to get unstuck.

God has always spoken to me through nature—sunsets, crashing waves, fields of grass, or any other beautiful thing He has made. The book of Job puts this perfectly:

> But ask the animals, and they will teach you,
>> or the birds in the sky, and they will tell you;
> or speak to the earth, and it will teach you,
>> or let the fish in the sea inform you.
> Which of all these does not know
>> that the hand of the LORD has done this?
> In his hand is the life of every creature
>> and the breath of all mankind. (Job 12:7–10)

So when I first landed in the beautiful state of Colorado, a place teeming with natural beauty, I was able to breathe deeply and welcome God's powerful yet calming presence. The crisp, cool air felt so pure in my lungs, and the mountains around us seemed hand-painted. I was not exactly excited about the emotional work to come, but I was grateful for the glorious setting—a backdrop to remind me that the great Maker of the universe held me in the palm of His hand.

The first week of therapy was . . . well, not easy. I began by dredging up the past and hashing out anything and everything that had ever hurt me. In my journal, I literally listed every person or situation I could remember that had ever brought me pain. Others' words, my own damaging thoughts, and people's actions were all listed on the page. Then my counselor had me write down any emotions I felt from those experiences as well as the lies I believed about myself because of them. By the end of our third day, I was totally out of sorts. I was exhausted from reliving every memory that had plagued my soul with heartache for so many years.

> I was exhausted from reliving every memory that had plagued my soul with heartache for so many years.

Pete was my therapist at Crossroads, and we had daily one-on-one sessions over the course of my stay. As we walked through my recorded memories together, Pete would pray with me and ask the Holy Spirit to take me back to those moments for even deeper healing. During one such prayer, I was carried back to myself at eight or nine years old. I was walking down the driveway to my old home where I grew up. The vision filled me with nostalgia, but it also filled me with an old shame. As a child,

I would look at that trailer and worry I didn't have friends because of it. I felt embarrassed and so alone. But in this return to the past—more than twenty years later—Jesus was there with me, taking in the scene as well. He was with me, then *and* now. Jesus can exist in our memories with us because He stands outside of time.

As this vision filled my mind, I had the warmest feeling I have ever felt. Jesus stood there with me in front of my home, but we didn't need to speak. In fact, nothing else mattered at that point. Then He reached toward my chest through skin and bones and cupped His hands around my heart. He literally held my heart in His hands, and I felt an impenetrable warmth all around it. I wanted to ask why He let certain things happen to me, but all that mattered in that moment was His presence. I was focused on Him holding my heart. I don't think I've ever felt so much protection.

For days, Pete and I went through every instance of hurt that I could remember and sat in prayer until we heard what Jesus had to say on the matter. Where was He when it happened, and how did He feel about it? In those days of counseling, I could feel truth moving from my head to my heart. The transformation had begun.

* * *

Pete walked with me through traumatic childhood dreams, painful experiences from grade school, and, of course, the damage done at the church I attended during my high school years. We pulled out memories I never would have thought about again, only to discover that they had been central to my ongoing struggles. Many of them pointed to the same nagging thought: the deep-seated, exhausting belief that God couldn't possibly love me. When I was a child, I was too poor. When I was a teenager, I was too evil. When I was an adult, I was too needy or too much. All of these things had been spoken over me

> How could He, the Creator of the universe, care for a creature like me?

at one time or another, and I'd reflected them back to God. How could He, the Creator of the universe, care for a creature like me?

This is what brought Pete and me outside to gaze at a mountaintop. For days we had been tilling the soil of my heart, asking God to reveal not only Himself but also my deepest, most secret wounds. And as that perfect, breathtaking sun sank farther and farther below the horizon line before me, I felt God planting a new seed.

Pete asked me the pivotal question: "As beautiful as that sunset is, God thinks you are even more beautiful than that. Do you believe it?"

Everything had led to this moment. So many tears and so much pain, so many disappointments and doubts.

God, is it true? Am I beautiful in Your sight? This time, can I really and truly trust You? Am I worthy of Your love?

I opened my eyes and opened my heart. Listened for the words that would change my world forever.

Yes, Tasha, it's true. You are beautiful. You are My masterpiece. I see you, and I know you. I love you. You are My child.

I inhaled a deep breath of cool Colorado air. As that truth finally started to take root in my soul—as the knowledge of God's unconditional love moved from my head to my heart—everything changed. It had not been clear until that moment that a great gap had existed between my formal beliefs and my functional beliefs. To accept that God loved me unconditionally—to truly *believe* it in my heart of hearts—would change the course of my existence. While previously I would have told people that God loved me, I hadn't been living that way. In fact, I had been living as if God loved everyone *but* me.

* * *

One of the things Pete taught me at Crossroads was the practice of healing prayer. Though it's a multistep, ancient practice worth researching in a far deeper way, I'll describe it briefly here. As Pete and I systematically examined the painful memories I'd conjured up, he invited me to pray over them and ask God where He was when each of those events took place. Then I would listen for His answer, for any message He wanted to send me regarding those devastating moments.

God, where were You when I had that terrifying nightmare?

God, where were You when I was locked alone in the bathroom all day, humiliated and afraid?

God, where were You when that woman at church said those horrible things about me even though I was so devoted to You?

God, where were You when I tried to end my life?

The process involved me waiting for God to speak to me through my imagination. It forced me to open my heart to Him, to allow Him to take control of my mind and redraw the memories that had held me captive. As I asked Him each question, I began to envision His presence in every wretched moment I'd experienced. Though I'd felt so alone, He'd been there. He had been with me through each devastating moment, cradling me in His arms.

As I mentioned, the healing prayer process involves many other steps that you may find worth exploring. But the point is about making time and room for heart-level conversations with God. It demands vulnerability and a willingness to address deep wounds that we'd often rather bandage superficially. But as I learned the power of healing prayer from Pete, I found myself returning to it again and again. The process is *that* powerful, but it's God's power that makes the practice meaningful and real.

I still had (and still have) work to do, but since that day on the mountaintop, I have felt more freedom than I ever previously understood to be possible. I have felt less lonely and been less critical of myself. I discovered that so much of what happened in my youth became the foggy lens through which I saw the entire world. I've been more honest with people and have worried less about their individual judgments. I try to be more vulnerable, and when I'm tempted to put on a façade, I remember that God doesn't want that for me. Then I take those lessons and apply them to others too. Each of us is a masterpiece to Him, and we ought to see and treat each other (and ourselves!) that way.

If you are feeling stuck today, I encourage you to schedule some quality time with God. Ask Him to reveal your wounds to you, and He can bind them up. Ask Him to expose your pain to the healing light of His truth. As Paul wrote to the Ephesians, God is "able to do immeasurably more than all we ask or imagine, according to his power that is at work within us" (Ephesians 3:20). There is freedom, and there is hope—but we must let Him in, let Him love us. I want you to know that joy waits for you on the other side, and Jesus lived, died, and rose again to make the journey with you.

But [God] said to me, "My grace is sufficient for you, for my power is made perfect in weakness." Therefore I will boast all the more gladly of my weaknesses, so that the power of Christ may rest upon me. For the sake of Christ, then, I am content with weaknesses, insults, hardships, persecutions, and calamities. For when I am weak, then I am strong.

—2 Corinthians 12:9–10 ESV

QUESTIONS TO CONSIDER

1. What are some of the breakthrough moments in your life when God made His presence most known to you?
2. When is the last time you spoke to God about the most persistent problems in your life? What has He revealed to you through these prayers?
3. Describe a moment when you realized you weren't practicing what you preached. What was the difference between what you knew to be true and what you felt in your heart?

Chapter 16

NASHVILLE

After my breakthrough at Crossroads, I felt invigo-
rated. When you feel loved and valued, you feel
infused with hope—and when you feel God's love con-
suming you from the inside out, you feel like a superhero!
At least, that's how I felt. Rather than being paralyzed by
an infinite number of options for my future, I was energized by the possibilities.

For some time I had toyed with the idea of moving to
Nashville, home to so much of the Christian publishing
and music industries. I wasn't looking for the spotlight at
all; in fact, I'd already seen firsthand the hiccups and haz-
ards that tend to accompany fame, so I would be fine just
doing my own thing, thank you. I had no job, no place
to live, and no real sense of what "moving to Nashville"
would look like in a literal sense. But since I was feeling

confident and experiencing this new level of divine freedom, I figured God would work out the details.

So I went. I packed up my little life and headed to Music City, USA, also known as Nashvegas, the Songwriting Capital of the World, and the Buckle of the Bible Belt. I wondered if I could find a writing job somewhere—maybe books or other Christian resources on topics like worship or prayer—though no job opening like that had appeared to me yet. When I needed money, maybe I could do some session singing on the side. The future seemed wide open and unpredictable, but I welcomed that.

My friend Ashley was kind enough to let me stay with her until I found a place of my own, and before long, I was working at a marketing job in town. Though I was grateful for the income, talk about a strange transition. To go from nonstop touring to nine-to-five desk work was weird, to say the least.

Once I had established myself a bit in Nashville, I got a call to sing on a track for a producer in town. He and I had planned to meet up within a couple of weeks anyway, but then he called and invited me to dinner after learning that I was new in town. I thought, *Why the heck not? I need new friends in Nashville!*

As I was getting dressed and ready that night, a quiet voice entered my mind.

You're going to meet your husband.

As much as I've endorsed listening for God's voice, I'll be honest: I brushed this one off. I shoved it aside, convincing myself it was just a passing thought.

Keith rolled up to my place in a car I thought was a little flashy. He also looked a little flashy himself: shiny shoes, a beautiful coat, and surprisingly long eyelashes. It's funny the things you remember, right? He was tall and gentlemanly, but he didn't seem like my type aside from those luscious eyelashes. Had you told me then we'd be engaged a year later, I might not have believed it.

* * *

Remember my five-year plan? The one that was so fantastically out of alignment with God's plan *and* reality? You might remember that "Find a husband" and "Marry him" were two of my unchecked items on that list—as if finding a partner for life is just a little task to do and be done with. I look back on that time and have such grace for myself and my expectations. It can be so frustrating to find peace in the moments when you can't see what God is up to, but hindsight is twenty-twenty *and* a delight. Living long enough to see what God has done is an enormous blessing.

By the time I met Keith, I'd been through some failed relationships and a broken engagement. At times I had wondered if it would ever happen for me at all, because I'd assumed I would meet my husband by my late twenties. The thoughts on the subject that constantly plagued me weren't healthy or rational ones. I would ask God, *What did I do to deserve this loneliness? Why are You withholding one of the most important things I desire in life?* I wondered if God was punishing me for something or if I wasn't good enough to deserve happiness— a damaging lie that I worked hard to rout out in my therapy program. What I didn't know yet was that God had something better. Once again, it was so much better than my own plan.

> It can be so frustrating to find peace in the moments when you can't see what God is up to, but hindsight is twenty-twenty *and* a delight.

I wrote my song "Thank You for the No" with Keith, Andrew Bergthold, and Tony Wood about this very thing: my tendency to doubt God in the waiting time. Though He has a full view of what we need and how our lives are going to play out, we still wonder about His methods and intentions. Here's how the chorus goes:

> Thank You for the not yet
> Thank You for the not now
> For the hold on, for the silence
> It took a while to see
> How You were saving me for something
> A little farther down the road
> Now I'm standing in Your better yes
> So thank You for the no

I would not be the wife and mother I am now without that time of forging my faith through trial, waiting, and heartbreak. Sure, some people get married and start families much younger, but that wasn't right for me—and God knew it. I spent so many years tormented by the lies I believed about myself

While my plan was to have it my way, His plan was carefully orchestrated and perfectly timed.

that I wonder how on earth I could've been as present and capable for others as I am now. By no stretch am I saying I'm perfect at either job—heaven knows I'm not!—but

I am grateful that Keith and I were led to each other at a time when my identity and my relationship with God were stronger.

Additionally, how lucky am I that I was able to see the world in my twenties, when I was healthy and energetic and fully able to physically enjoy the excitement? From a young age, I always had a wanderlust, and God granted me such a gift in satisfying much of that. Sometimes when I think about all the cool places I've been able to go, I feel like I've lived ten lives. While my plan was to have it my way, His plan was carefully orchestrated and perfectly timed. It may seem frivolous to some, but I needed to do things like skydive, backpack through India, bungee jump off bridges, and dive in Iceland. I did them all. How incredible that God was satisfying that longing for adventure in my heart, even when I didn't fully understand what He was doing.

God's timing is, indeed, perfect. And His no today may just lead you to a much more beautiful yes.

> God's timing is, indeed, perfect. And His no today may just lead you to a much more beautiful yes.

He has made everything beautiful in its time. He has also set eternity in the human heart; yet no one can fathom what God has done from beginning to end.
—Ecclesiastes 3:11

QUESTIONS TO CONSIDER

1. Have you experienced a failed relationship that prepared you for a more permanent relationship later on? Or what have you learned from certain friendships that you've carried forward?

2. How has God proven to you that His timing is perfect? Describe a moment when something you wanted didn't occur, but God was looking out for you with His response to your prayers.

3. Describe a moment when you felt God leading you somewhere though you weren't sure why. Did you follow His urging? What was the outcome?

Chapter 17

SONGWRITING

When I moved to Nashville, I'd only dabbled in songwriting, despite all my years performing. Then one morning, I woke up, heard something from God, and hit my husband with this idea:

"Keith, I think the Lord told me to try writing some songs."

Keith's a crazy good musician, if you didn't know already. He plays tons of instruments, produces music, and has been a long-standing member of DiverseCity with TobyMac. He's also won some impressive awards like GRAMMYs and Doves, though he'd never brag about that. It's fun to be married to a person who shares a love for music with me and supports my career—including the moments when God just suggests I try something totally new.

So we began to write.

When I played with songwriting in the past, I let my instincts drive the truck. Composing was more of an expressive practice for me, and I found it to be a freeing process. I didn't really even know there were "rules" to writing music until I moved to Nashville and learned about them from people in the industry.

At one point in my life, I might've considered myself disadvantaged because I didn't know what was in the songwriting playbook. The perpetual student in me probably would've ordered every book on the subject and tried to catch up on what I'd missed. But as Keith and I experimented, I felt once again that God could use my weakness as a strength. I approached the process with a unique mindset, and since I didn't even know what the rules were, I felt free to break them! I've learned so much from industry professionals over the years, and I'm grateful to every person who has collaborated with me. But I hope I can always maintain a distinctive outlook on the music we are making.

Around that time, I was helping lead worship for a conference at Church of the City, and a man approached me backstage.

"You're really anointed to lead worship," he said. "What are you doing with your life?"

Good question, sir!

I told him I led worship regularly at Church of the City but that I also had a marketing job in town. He asked me if I'd be interested in grabbing a cup of coffee. And since he had a fancy-sounding British accent, I said yes.

Keith and I met up with him that week, knowing little about this man. During our conversation, Keith mentioned that we had been writing songs together, and as we were leaving, the man asked to hear some of them. We obliged, thinking little of the encounter, assuming this was just a friendly gentleman from church.

As it turned out, the guy worked for an imprint called BEC at a label named Tooth & Nail. A few months later, I had a record deal.

I'm telling you, no one was more shocked by this than me. I had *never* aspired to become an "artist." To be honest, sometimes I still have trouble calling myself an artist or hearing others describe me as one! I had already seen firsthand what fame could do to people, and I did not want a part of that. In fact, I had been just fine leading worship, as I had done happily for years and years. The idea of recording a record and then performing it gave me a lot of pause, so I needed some arm-twisting.

God had to work that out in my heart, mainly through my husband. Keith reminded me that God had opened this door, not us. We hadn't gone looking for the opportunity; we'd just tried to live obediently and followed the voice that told me to give writing a shot. For some time, I wrestled with it and prayed over my decisions. It became clear that God was doing something, and I shouldn't be fighting it.

My first single, "Love Lifting Me," came out in 2018, and the *Love Running Wild* EP came out the next year. Suddenly I had a career in singing and songwriting—not at all what I'd planned to do when I moved to Nashville! Three more EPs and a studio album later, I guess this is my job now. Sometimes it hardly seems real to me. I look up and around and ask, *God, how did You do all this?*

> It became clear that God was doing something, and I shouldn't be fighting it.

What I do now feels so different from the touring I did years ago—and that's because we *planned* to do it differently. Every choice we make is purposeful and prayer-covered. It takes a village to keep an operation like this running, and I hope every person I get to work with feels like an integral part of the team rather than a secondary support. We make things happen *together*, and I couldn't do anything without them. God put us all in the same place for a reason, and I don't want any of us to lose sight of that.

I also want to foster a work environment where people can check me. I had a manager early on who used to carry my bags or open doors for me often. And maybe he was trying to be gentlemanly, but sometimes a woman needs to carry her own bags to keep herself grounded. "Your job is to be honest with me about my career," I told him. "It's not to be a yes-man or to puff me up. And when you are trying to blow smoke, I can see right through it. Just FYI!" He couldn't help but laugh, and I still lug my own suitcases around (although I'll gladly accept help now when I'm tired).

What keeps us going, though, is the ministry. We've never lost sight of the main thing, which is worshiping God and shar-ing our love for Him with whoever will listen. Without setting that intention, it could be so easy to run right off

> It's as if God's hands are all over the infrastructure, making sure the right people are involved and the tracks are laid before the train arrives.

the tracks. We could get caught up in busyness, jump at every opportunity, and move at a pace that leaves little room for reflection and prayer over our work. I'm grateful that we've made time for what matters and things have kept moving at a manageable pace. It's as if God's hands are all over the infrastructure, making sure the right people are involved and the tracks are laid before the train arrives.

Therefore, I urge you, brothers and sisters, in view of God's mercy, to offer your bodies as a living sacrifice, holy and pleasing to God—this is your true and proper worship. Do not conform to the pattern of this world, but be transformed by the renewing of your mind. Then you will be able to test and approve what God's will is—his good, pleasing and perfect will.
—Romans 12:1–2

QUESTIONS TO CONSIDER

1. Have you ever had the urge to try something brand-new? What was it, and did you follow through with it?

2. Who are the people in your life who keep you grounded? What honest conversations have you had in the past to keep each other accountable?

3. Has God ever sent you down a path you weren't sure about? How did He make His will known to you in that moment?

Chapter 18

VOICE

For a little while, when I was dating Keith, I taught voice and theology at Trevecca University, a Nazarene school in Nashville. Having loved school so much, this felt like a natural path for me.

If you've ever taught students or younger people, you know that teaching forces you to clarify a lot of your own thoughts and ideas. One of the key things I used to tell my students is that the human voice is a changeable thing, and as you grow as a singer, you grow as a person. That had been my experience, at least, and I wanted my students to grow spiritually as they grew into their talent.

So much had opened up for me since my two weeks at Crossroads. I found lightness in everything I did, and the freedom I felt infiltrated every corner of my life. My singing voice changed as well. For the longest time, it had remained bridled and controlled. I rarely took risks, and I stayed within the boundaries of what I knew I could do. But as I grew and healed, and as God ripped up the lies that had once been written on my heart, my voice grew stronger. I started trying new things and realized that I was more capable than I'd ever known. What came out of my mouth was suddenly a much truer expression of who I was and who God wanted me to become— all because I felt free.

> But as I grew and healed, and as God ripped up the lies that had once been written on my heart, my voice grew stronger.

Singing was just one reflection of everything going on inside of me. I discovered myself unconcerned about making musical mistakes in front of audiences, and I grew more confident in my everyday choices. So what if I hit a flat note once in a while? It stopped mattering as much to me because one wonky note wasn't going to be the end of the world. And it most certainly wasn't what defined me. Overall, I worried less and less about how I was perceived by others in every other arena of my life. What mattered to me was God's opinion—and feeling supported, known, and loved by Him allowed me to feel freedom as I poured my heart out in song.

As my career in Christian music kicked into gear in Nashville, I attributed any forward movement to this God-given freedom and the knowledge that I couldn't do *any* of it without Him. And I didn't want to. I knew that without His presence, any "wins" I experienced would be for naught. A good song or a good singer wouldn't ever break a yoke on someone's life on its own; only God's anointing over a song or a singer could turn an experience holy.

Letting God be in control of my career and voice produced another surprising result: I no longer felt pressure like I once did. When I was singing on stage with Katy or in session recordings in Los Angeles, the performance anxiety could take its toll because mistakes might cost me a job or my career. That mental space is exhausting, no matter what kind of professional pressure you're under. Imagine my relief when I realized that it was *God's* promise to save me, and I couldn't even save myself if I tried. Releasing my music into His hands left me feeling lighter, less worried, and freer to experiment. He was in charge of every ounce of it, and I could finally breathe.

* * *

For several months, I had been leading worship occasionally at a large church in the Midwest. On a contract basis, they would fly me up on certain weekends, and then I'd go home to Nashville after services. Eventually, the church asked if I'd be up for something more permanent, and I flew up for the weekend to sing for an official audition.

Halfway through a song, my voice just crumpled. I couldn't stay on pitch or ever find it again. Missing notes here and there is normal, but this was not. Stunned, I walked off the platform.

As soon as I was backstage, Keith rushed toward me and took me by the shoulders. "Honey, I have *never* heard you sound like that," he said. "That was terrible. What happened out there?"

Keith is always honest with me, OK? He doesn't hold back, and I love him for it.

"I have no idea!" I told him. "But I had no control over my voice." It was unlike anything I had ever felt before.

My mind began spinning. As you can imagine, losing your voice is a singer's nightmare. I had already lost my voice once, back in high school when I was removed from leading worship. For so long, I had given it up, and for years afterward I had fought to get it back. I'd felt stronger, more confident, and more creatively free than I had in so long. Was I going to have to give it up again?

My vocal training had been strong, so I knew I wasn't short on technique. I knew how to sing properly and had always taken the correct measures to protect and maintain my voice. I made healthy choices and didn't abuse my assets. Yet the problem persisted, and I was yet again faced with my least favorite feeling: lacking control.

I wondered if something else was just catching up with me. Heck, I even wondered if I'd inhaled too much stage fog and glitter from the Katy Perry tour. (File that one under "Things only Tasha might wonder.") Having no answers, I made an appointment at Vanderbilt Voice Center to see what they could figure out.

The clinicians scoped my throat and discovered that I was in a prenodule phase. Nodules are bad news for singers. They're basically benign bumps that form on the vocal cords, a bit like calluses. They can be caused by a variety of things, though it wasn't quite clear what was causing mine. All we knew was that my vocal cords were severely inflamed and demanding I give them a break.

One cause of nodules is allergies, which was something I'd never really dealt with before. So I went for allergy testing and learned that I'm basically allergic to everything in Nashville's air. (It's a real mystery how Nashville, a veritable hotbed for allergens, somehow became a music mecca for thousands of singers—but that's a whole other conversation.) This was a brand-new problem for me, so the next few months were about learning how to take care of my voice despite the airborne mold and pollen that had been taking a toll on my body. I started some vocal therapy after several months of rest. But as I started singing again, I felt myself reverting to the place where my voice had bottomed out.

Fortunately, I found a vocal coach who taught me some specific techniques for training and protecting my voice. I got on allergy meds, changed my diet, and continued to see some forward progress. By this time I'd been signed by my label, so even more was at stake. Then at a show in Phoenix, my voice went wonky once again.

A good friend in Phoenix got me an appointment with the best ENT in town. This was starting to feel like an emergency. The scope showed similar severe inflammation, which was frustrating considering all the rehab I'd done and life changes I'd made. The doctor wound up prescribing me a nasal spray that has really improved

> Those stressful months really took a toll on my heart and mind.

my allergy issues, and I've maintained a complicated but effective "voice protection regimen" ever since. It's not exactly easy to keep up, but I'm beyond grateful that I've found solutions. I'm just doing what needs to be done.

Those stressful months really took a toll on my heart and mind. Things would start to move for me professionally, only for me to be knocked back down again whenever my voice would crack. I had finally found my voice, the tool that God seemed to have provided me to share what was in my heart, only to discover how precarious a tool it really was. I returned to the prayer method I had learned years before in Colorado: the healing prayer of asking, *God, where are You in this? What happens next if I never sing again?*

Not being able to rely on my voice was challenging, but through prayer, I remembered that the only thing I can really rely on is God. I can faithfully take the necessary steps to protect myself, but I've had to surrender everything, including my voice, to God. If He wants me to sing, then I will. And if the day comes that He doesn't want that for me anymore, then I'll be at peace with it.

A lot of singers find their identity in what they can do. And that's not limited to musicians; all kinds of people root their purpose in their professions or talents. As I contemplated the what-ifs when it came to possibly losing my voice, I was grateful that I'd never found my identity in music. Yes, it's something I have done passionately for years, and I've put a lot of stock in it. But at the end of the day, what matters most is that I belong to God.

Though I love to sing, I don't live for it. I live to see people changed. God can use me whether I sing or not, just as He can use anyone for any of His chosen purposes. It's not always effortless, but all we need to do is welcome Him to take the reins and invite Him into the choices we make. And more often than not, if we loosen our grips on the things we think we need, He will map out journeys for us that are more grand than what we would have ever designed for ourselves.

Stop and consider God's wonders.
Do you know how God controls the clouds
and makes his lightning flash?
Do you know how the clouds hang poised,
those wonders of him who has perfect knowledge?
—Job 37:14–16

QUESTIONS TO CONSIDER

1. How does it feel to release something into God's hands? What can you release to Him today that has been causing you grief or stress?

2. Do you find yourself identifying too much with one of your life's roles (for example, a career or a relationship)? What happens when those roles eclipse our identities as God's beloved children?

3. Describe a moment when you felt completely out of control. How did you respond to what was happening? How could you have handled it better or differently?

Chapter 19

HOPE

When Keith and I got married, we knew two things about our family: one, that we wanted kids, and two, that it would be hard for us to have them. We talked a lot about adoption and had planned on something like that for the future. We looked forward to bringing children into our home in whatever way God would allow.

Keith already knew that having children would be nearly impossible. He had been married before and knew from past testing that infertility was an issue for him. Doctors told us it was most likely due to a back injury he sustained years ago. The injury resulted in regular pain—a battle he had to endure almost daily. Though he'd known about his infertility, emotions resurfaced when our union became real. He knew plenty of other people who had experienced infertility, so he'd witnessed their struggles up close too. But suddenly it hit home again and affected him in ways he didn't expect. He asked questions like, "What would it say about *God* if He *couldn't* heal me? What would it say about *me* if He *wouldn't*? Would I be a bad dad?"

As we planned for our future and began talking more about adoption, though, I had this feeling in my gut that we would have a biological child. I knew the facts, but these thoughts kept stirring in my mind. I wondered why God was letting my mind even go there if the door to pregnancy was closed. One day while I was praying I heard the Lord say, "It will be a sign to him."

> I wondered why God was letting my mind even go there if the door to pregnancy was closed.

When I hesitantly expressed these thoughts to Keith, I don't think I fully understood how they would affect him too. He already bore the weight of our struggle, and my hopeful words seemed to put more pressure on him. While I was hoping for a miracle, he was feeling like a failure. My intent was never to hurt him, of course, but my words stung him nonetheless.

I continued to pray and listen to the voice telling me not to give up. I prayed for Keith and told him I was doing so. Before long, his heart began to shift as well. He understood that I was not setting him up for failure but lifting him up to God as the man I loved, the future father of my children. At one point, he discovered that he had embraced a sliver of hope for himself.

* * *

At the beginning of 2016, we sat down together to make a list of our yearly goals. (You know I love a list!) But this time, our list must have been a little tame because a voice whispered to me, "You and Keith can do all of this on your own, Tasha. You don't need me for any of this." I think God was urging us to lean into His power and believe for what actually required faith . . . things that would sting if they didn't come to pass. Things that would hurt. So we added three big things: first, a new house; second, a trip to Africa; and third, a child. Each of them felt like a stretch.

To be honest, after that day, we didn't really attend to that list very faithfully. We just wrote down our items and went about our business. The day-to-day routine carried on while that list remained ideas written on a page. So nothing that happened afterward was due to our effort or attention!

That summer, a friend reached out and asked us to come to Uganda to teach music at a worship camp called Watoto Children's Village. We hadn't made any effort to travel to Africa since we'd made our list, mostly because a trip like that wasn't within our financial budget. The opportunity came to us anyway, and to ice the cake, our friend told us our expenses would be paid. Keith had never traveled to Africa before, and since Africa holds such a special place in my heart, I believed a trip there would bring us closer in our relationship. Because it's my happy place, I thought he would know me better by going. We were elated. "Sign us both up!" we told our friend. We soon packed up and headed to Uganda.

As we taught alongside other musicians at worship camp and observed the talent of the wonderful kids at Watoto, we were thankful for the invitation. I had wanted Keith to experience Africa in person, and I was beyond grateful for us to see Uganda together. Watoto is so special because the children who live there are all adopted into families made up of widows. James 1:27 tells us, "Religion that God our Father accepts as pure and faultless is this: to look after orphans and widows in their distress and to keep oneself from being polluted by the world." The church at Watoto does this in the most literal way.

One night during worship with the students, Keith's pain was severe. As we traveled, he'd slept on some uncomfortable beds that had aggravated his back. He couldn't get comfortable while playing his instrument, so he got down on his knees. We were leading the song "Miracles" by Jesus Culture, and I looked over to my right to see Keith bent down and weeping.

Later he told me that in his efforts to get comfortable, he decided to pray. He set his trumpet in front of him on the floor and spoke to God. Within an instant, his discomfort disappeared. Still on the ground, he shifted and twisted and felt absolutely no pain—a relief he had not felt for years. He felt in that moment that his suffering had been taken from him.

When I saw him weeping to my right, he was realizing that his pain had been lifted away. He stood up and told me, "Tasha, I think God just healed my back." And to this day, his pain has never returned. That same night, as our team gathered to debrief and prepare for the next day, someone asked if they could pray for us to have a child. They surrounded us and lifted us up in prayer. As they did, I couldn't help but remember another trip to Africa and another blessing I'd received. Just as the women of Kenya had spoken motherhood into my future identity, so did the wonderful people I'd met in Uganda.

* * *

When we got back to Tennessee, God officially answered another of our prayers. He had already been at work on finding us a home before our trip, but it all became final once we were back on US soil. I knew God's hand was all over it because not only had He directed us to a home, but He'd also found us one with two walk-in closets in the primary bedroom. (I'm kidding! Sort of. . . .) We were enormously blessed to have a home at all, and considering the challenging market in and around Nashville, we felt even *more* fortunate to have a comfortable place to call home.

As we were moving, Keith seemed to be in rare form. He was lifting boxes and furniture that would have previously posed problems for him. I looked at him and asked, "How's your back holding up over there?" I didn't want him to lift too much and hurt himself again.

"It's never felt better," he told me. As he continued to test his physical limits with the heavier boxes, it became more real for us that his back might be fully healed, for good. How incredible that God had taken care of two of our three big-picture dreams in a matter of weeks, and to top it off, He'd drastically changed my husband's life.

By December, we had settled in nicely to our home. The year had been full of ups and downs, but God had done amazing things for us. With two weeks left in the year, we went to lunch with a pastor and were updating him on those highs and lows. "God's score is two for three right now!" we joked. Keith still seemed slightly hesitant to hope too hard for a child, but deep inside, I was holding out for a miracle. Little did we know that as we were speaking those words, God had already accomplished his third mission. I was pregnant.

I had spent the first weeks of December feeling a bit uncomfortable, but I'd chalked it up to all the travel we'd been doing. *I'm just exhausted*, I told myself. *Nothing to see here.* Then one night right before Christmas, I decided to take a pregnancy test—you know, just in case.

I took the test and set the timer. When I heard the *beep* and came to look at the results, they read negative. Disappointed as usual, I released the breath I'd been holding and went about my night. I left the stick on the counter, then walked past it again ten minutes later. I looked down.

Positive?

My breath hitched. *What on earth?* I'd followed the directions on the box to the letter, so why would this little stick-test thingy change its mind ten minutes later? I fumbled around and tried another test, and the same thing happened: negative, then positive, but ten minutes later than the timer. As any normal, red-blooded, American woman would do, I hit up Google. The internet told me to try again in the morning.

Sleep didn't come easily that night. Then early in the morning, I went to the store while Keith was still sleeping and bought seven different kinds of tests. I came home and quietly hid in the bathroom. The first test I took produced the same late result as the ones from the night before, so I decided to try a different brand.

This one was positive—right on the money, right on time.

I couldn't believe it, so I took another test.

Another positive.

I holed up in that bathroom long enough to go through all seven of the tests that I bought, and each one told me the same thing: I was pregnant. I called the doctor for even more confirmation. "Hello, this is Tasha Layton Smith. I've just taken seven pregnancy tests that all came out positive. Could this be a mistake? Is it possible I'm *not* pregnant?"

> This one was positive—right on the money, right on time.

"No, ma'am," the nurse told me. "The odds of that would be like winning the lottery."

Shock set in. I had to not only process this news but also figure out how to tell Keith. I couldn't wait. I was so thankful to God, not just for this little one I hadn't even met yet, but also for His faithfulness. He had come through after all. Three for three.

Since Christmas was around the corner, I put all the pregnancy tests into a little Christmas stocking and hung it on the mantel. Keith's stocking waited up there with mine and our dog Dexter's. As soon as Keith woke up I could barely contain myself, so I dragged him downstairs and told him to look inside. Later he told me he was worried about what was happening because my face looked pale and I was acting so weird!

When he first peeked inside the stocking, he wasn't quite sure what the pregnancy tests were. He was probably still half-asleep too, which didn't help the situation. He pulled out one of the sticks and examined it. Then he looked up, and our eyes met. It finally clicked.

We were both so flooded with emotion that we just held each other and cried. It was the happy kind of cry, the cry of so much gratitude. So many tears were shed that miracle-filled Christmas.

* * *

Hope seems to get a bad rap sometimes, as if people think of it as the opposite of action. But I don't think that's a fair take. Hope isn't just a fuzzy feeling. Hope is about believing in the possibility of something wonderful or miraculous taking place—about opening one's heart to the greatness to come. As believers, we hope for Christ's return. We hope for an eternity with God. But as we wait for God's will to be done, we experience the gifts accompanying a hopeful heart. The apostle Paul wrote to the Romans, "May the God of hope fill you with all joy and peace in believing, so that by the power of the Holy Spirit you may abound in hope" (Romans 15:13 ESV). Hope enables us to envision a brighter future—and the outflow of hope is the gift of peace in the time of waiting and anticipating.

When Keith and I presented God with our deepest desires, He not only gave them to us but also addressed the healing that needed to take place. He went above and beyond our asking because that is who He is: a generous and loving Father. Isaiah 40:31 is a favorite verse for many because it captures the power of God and our hope in Him. The Scripture says, "Those who hope in the LORD will renew their strength. They will soar on wings like eagles; they will run and not grow weary, they will walk and not be faint."

I want that for all of us today—to feel the wind carrying us higher and higher. God *is* good. God *is* faithful. And He will renew all things in their time.

If you are feeling hopeless today, believe me when I say I've been there. I've felt despair and wondered where God could possibly be amid my pain. But I can also tell you that God *will* show up in ways even bigger than our imaginings. Your struggles today will almost certainly become your strength tomorrow. And though Jesus never promised that each of our days would be easy, He did promise to be with us always.

> God *is* good. God *is* faithful. And He will renew all things in their time.

Jesus also didn't promise that we would get exactly what we ask for. In fact, He told us, "In this world you will have trouble. But take heart! I have overcome the world" (John 16:33). You may not understand God's timing or actions, but He will not let you down. I encourage you to try hope on for size. Be bold in your requests to God and hold out for miracles. He's brought me out of places I thought I would never escape, and He can do the same for you.

> *Show me your ways, LORD,*
> *teach me your paths.*
> *Guide me in your truth and teach me,*
> *for you are God my Savior,*
> *and my hope is in you all day long.*
> *Remember, LORD, your great mercy and love,*
> *for they are from of old.*
> —Psalm 25:4–6

QUESTIONS TO CONSIDER

1. What is the purpose of hope? How does it play a role in your life and mindset?

2. Why do you think we are sometimes afraid to hope for things? What relationship does hope have to disappointment?

3. What is the boldest thing you have ever asked God for? How did He respond to your request?

Chapter 20

BIRTH PAINS

Can I be honest? Being pregnant was miserable. All you women who enjoyed every blissful moment of your pregnancy? I wish I could understand! Though I was beyond overjoyed to be carrying a baby—a miracle, as far as I was concerned—I was sick as a dog. Morning sickness, sore back, swollen limbs, acid reflux . . . oh, the acid reflux. Round ligament pain, insomnia, the impossibility of sleeping any decent length of time because I had to pee so much. It was bonkers how bad I felt. Maybe my hardship was because I was pregnant in my mid thirties instead of my mid twenties, or maybe I'm just lucky like that. Whatever the case, how had women throughout history gone through this year after year? Suddenly I had a new, mad respect for my species.

I was so ready for the pregnancy part to be over. In fact, the day before my due date, Keith and I took a long hike to see if it would kickstart my labor. That plan didn't work, though the hike did raise my blood pressure and help me gain some water weight. The doctor was worried about preeclampsia, so she admitted me for an induction.

I was excited and scared and nervous and every other emotion a soon-to-be mother feels. We were *finally* going to meet our son—our miracle baby!

I had prepared myself for a completely natural birth. When I arrived at the hospital, however, things didn't play out according to the birth plan I had discussed with my doctor. The nurses immediately hooked me up to a monitor and started an IV, which confined me to the bed. I was disappointed because I was worried about being able to manage the pain without walking or standing or sitting on the exercise ball.

> We were *finally* going to meet our son— our miracle baby!

Because I wanted a natural birth, the hospitalists began a low dose of Pitocin to start labor. We were all hoping my body would take over the process. Instead, we learned I did *not* respond well to the drug. They had to give me more and more, and I was eventually on the highest dosage without progress. The contractions were the most painful thing I'd ever experienced.

They broke my water, but that didn't help either. The narcotic they gave me didn't help me relax. I'd been in hard labor for over twenty-four hours by then, and I was loopy but still felt every bit of the pain. I had two options—epidural or C-section—and I was so tired I worried I wouldn't have the energy to push if labor continued to go this slowly. I was determined against surgery, however, so I kept struggling.

After several more hours, the doctor gave me an epidural, which was painful in and of itself! I was shaking from the pain and wondered how much more I could take. Eventually I was able to rest, and my body finally started making way for our baby. I woke up from a short nap only to feel nauseated, ready to throw up. Soon it was time to push.

For three and a half hours, I pushed and pushed. I was praying and asking for relief but finding little. What on earth was taking so long? As it turned out, our son had also become exhausted from the work of being born, so he'd just quit helping his mama out. The job was all up to me. I'd been laboring for two days with little sleep and no food. I finally told Keith that I didn't think I could do it anymore. But while I was feeling hopeless, Keith saw the baby's progress and encouraged me onward. After twenty minutes of believing I might die, our son, Levi, was finally born.

We chose our son's name quite carefully. In the Old Testament, Levi was the patriarch Jacob's third son, and the Tribe of Levi became the one responsible for all of Israel's priestly duties. The Levites had special status as well as special obligations, as they were tasked with maintaining and protecting the temple. Scripture is also filled with mentions of the Levites being singers and musicians. In other words, they were "set apart" for service and worship. Keith and I have always considered ourselves worship leaders above all else, and it was this shared love of worship music that brought us together in the first place. Our son's name is fitting because we hope he will inherit the love of music we plan to keep alive in our home, but also because we believe he is set apart and will find and pursue his own calling.

Maybe becoming a parent is part of your calling. Maybe your calling is about encouraging others, sharing the gospel, leading worship at church, or something else entirely. Whatever it may be, I guarantee that the journey to and through your calling will make for a rocky road at times. Nothing about being a mother has been easy for me, except for the part where I automatically and immediately loved my kids. From the moments when I hoped for them, through the moments I prayed for them, through the moments I carried and birthed them, and now as I am raising them—each of these steps has been (and will continue to be) filled with trials. But in my experience, nothing worth doing isn't hard-won. Jesus doesn't promise ease, but He does promise His presence. Hebrews 13:5 repeats a phrase that is present throughout Scripture: "Never will I leave you; never will I forsake you." That is the Lord's message to you and me.

As I struggled to give birth to my son, I also struggled to remember that God was with me in the room. But He was there then, and He is still with us today. Even though Jesus and I have history, I like to say, it would be wrong of me to pretend that I don't question God's plans or lose sight of His power from time to time. The hours and days after Levi's birth were also difficult, for reasons I will explain later—and those stressors resulted in a difficult spiritual moment for me too. But the thing is, God doesn't let go of us even

> Jesus doesn't promise ease, but He does promise His presence.

when we aren't quite sure if He's there. He is with us from our first breath to our last, from our lowest points to our highest.

I love to read the Psalms because they are beautiful, but I also appreciate how honest they are. The songs are filled with praise, but they also explore the full range of human emotion: anger, fear, joy, sadness, confusion, you name it. Psalm 42 is a wonderful example of this, as it begins with the poet's desperate longing for God. The words glorify God and His power, but then the writer's heart turns on a dime when he says,

> I say to God my Rock,
>   "Why have you forgotten me?
> Why must I go about mourning,
>   oppressed by the enemy?"
> My bones suffer mortal agony
>   as my foes taunt me,
> saying to me all day long,
>   "Where is your God?" (Psalm 42:9–10)

I can relate to the psalmist David feeling forgotten. But what I know now, more than ever, is that God is always near. He is always working on something, whether or not I can see it. The psalm ends with this directive: "Put your hope in God, for I will yet praise him, my

Savior and my God" (verse 11). Notice the word *yet*; though the psalmist may still be unsure of what God is up to, he chooses to praise Him anyway. God has proven Himself worthy of my trust over and over, and the longer I live, the more I get to see His hand at work. Even when I feel like the ground beneath me is shaky, it is my privilege to sing about the wonderful things God has done in the dark.

> Don't be afraid to ask God to reveal His presence to you if you are feeling forgotten or alone.

Don't be afraid to ask God to reveal His presence to you if you are feeling forgotten or alone. He will uncover Himself in His way and in His time. Don't be afraid to share your grievances with Him either because He already knows what they are. And if you are feeling unsure of your purpose or stuck in a spiritual desert, present your questions to the One who made you. Hang on for a little while longer. God will show up.

I took you from the ends of the earth,
from its farthest corners I called you.
I said, "You are my servant";
I have chosen you and have not rejected you.
So do not fear, for I am with you;
do not be dismayed, for I am your God.
I will strengthen you and help you;
I will uphold you with my righteous right hand.
—Isaiah 41:9–10

QUESTIONS TO CONSIDER

1. When have you felt most alone? Did you call out for God in those moments? Were you afraid?
2. If you have a favorite psalm from the Bible, name it. What emotions does it describe?
3. God already knows what's in your heart and mind. What in the past, if anything, has held you back from bringing your fears, frustrations, praise, or any other words to God?

Chapter 21

MAMA BEAR

When I first became a mom—when I first held my son, Levi—I thought he had the most beautiful eyes I'd ever seen. Keith and I had wanted him for so long, and when Levi finally looked up at me, newly born, an unfamiliar feeling came over me. Granted, it was a bit of shock and trauma at the long and painful birth we'd just endured, but the feeling was mixed with an overwhelming, crushing love. If you've ever given birth, my guess is you understand what a wild experience it is and how it changes you from the inside out. These days I'm a mama bear—a fierce version of myself that was hiding deep within. I didn't even know she was in there!

The hours before and after his birth were some of the most frightening I've ever experienced. My labor lasted for over thirty-three hours, and I lost a lot of blood in the process. Then, to make matters much worse, Levi came into the world without breath. I can barely describe the helplessness I felt as I watched my newborn son—the child I'd been praying for—fight for his life as the medical team resuscitated him. While Levi spent his first week in the NICU, I also struggled to recover and wound up needing surgery of my own. The combination of physical and emotional pain was almost too much for us to bear. Though I was grateful that Levi had survived, little else seemed to go right in those early days for our little family.

Gratitude for my son and the complications of my pregnancy continued to battle each other in the days and weeks that followed. Keith had to go back on tour soon after Levi was born, so I was doubly exhausted, overwhelmed, anxious, and depressed. Dealing with my emotional roller coaster was bad enough; doing it by myself felt near impossible. Frustrated, I'd ask God again, *Where are You in all of this? What am I supposed to be learning?* My questions seemed to be met with silence, and I felt desperately alone and afraid.

Sometimes, though, my prayers would be met with something worse than silence: I'd get exactly the opposite of what I prayed for! If I asked God to help Levi and me sleep, we'd spend the entire night up with crying and reflux. If I asked God to give me some pain relief, I'd be in more pain than before. After enough of this, I thought, *Why am I even praying at all?* A familiar distrust crept in, and I felt myself drifting further from God.

It took almost a year for me to be able to look back on the frightening days after Levi was born with any sort of clarity. Then one day, amid a courageous moment that can only be explained as grace-driven, I pulled out some photos from the day of Levi's birth. To that point, I'd been unable to look at them—unable to return to those terror-filled moments and the succeeding days and weeks when God seemed so far away. As I pored over these pictures for the first time and faced the deep well of my emotions, I returned to the healing prayer practices I'd learned years ago at Crossroads. Only then could I see clearly that God had protected Levi and me. He'd been with us all along.

> A familiar distrust crept in, and I felt myself drifting further from God.

Once again, the circumstances of Levi's birth and my recovery had seriously tested the limits of my control. And when things went haywire, I feared God had abandoned me. In fact, I'd begun to believe He had. But as I looked at the pictures of us and prayed over them, a spirit of peace moved over me, replacing the lie that God had betrayed my son and me. Though I'd let that lie take root, it was time to pull it up and sow a new seed. Yes, I had feared for my son's life and I had been in pain, but God had protected us both. He had managed just fine without me, and my trust in Him still had room to grow.

* * *

Becoming a parent has taught me more about God than anything I've ever done. For example, I knew God created me and felt unconditional love for me—but now, with this tiny, precious baby in my arms, I could understand the concept even more. Motherhood has also exposed my selfishness even more than my marriage has, but on the flip side, I'm reminded constantly that I would do absolutely anything for my kids.

> Becoming a parent has taught me more about God than anything I've ever done.

I'll never forget my first outing with just Levi and me. Keith was on the road, and I needed to do some shopping. Getting the baby in the car, driving down the road, taking the baby out of the car . . . these all seem like huge tasks for the first-time mom on her own. This was especially true for me after the trauma he and I had experienced together. Anyway, it was still warm outside, and as I was fastening Levi into his seat, a bee flew into the car.

The thing is, bees scare me. I absolutely hate the thought of being stung.

Before I knew what I was doing, I caught that bee with my bare hand—straight-up Mr. Miyagi-ed that deal. My protective instinct kicked in faster than my fear, and the whole of me said, *You will not try me, bug. I will die for this baby!*

I didn't have to die for my son that day (thank goodness), but God went and did just that for each of His children. Out of love, He created us, died for us, and rose again for us. And nothing we ever do can get in the way of that love. Romans 8:35 asks, "Who shall separate us from the love of Christ?" The short answer? Nothing.

After the bee debacle, I just sat in my car for a few moments and thought about everything that had changed in my heart. What more was I willing to do to protect my son? I'm not saying that only parents can understand God's love and sacrifice—that's certainly not the case!— but for me, some theoretical thoughts about God were simply becoming more real. And the things I was feeling about God were softening, even in the moments when

He felt so far away. They helped me understand that He is more of a good, kind, and patient Father than I'd imagined. And yet He is so much more than our imaginations can even fathom.

Parenting has also better helped me understand God's compassion. When my little ones mess up (all the time), I mostly think about how hard it must be to be small. Don't you think God thinks about us in a similar way? Good parents don't sit around waiting for mistakes, looking for opportunities to punish their children. God loves us because we're His, not because we're perfect. And when we do mess up, He wants to teach us through it and forgive us.

Christ came to earth and shared in our humanity so He could embody the same experiences we undertake each day. He went hungry, He grieved the dead, He got tired, and His friends disappointed Him. You name it, Jesus experienced it. Though our journey on earth is about getting closer to God and better understanding Him, He already understands you and me completely. He doesn't just count the hairs on our heads; He knows what it's like to *be* us.

Back when I was receiving therapy at Crossroads, one of the hard lessons I had to learn was about being gentle with myself the way God is gentle with us. Amid an inner healing prayer, it struck me that I needed to have compassion on myself in the same way I would have compassion on a little child.

When I considered my past and all the humiliating things I'd experienced, I only felt shame. But when I stepped outside myself and *then* looked back inward, I saw a broken, embarrassed little one who needed comfort and care—from me! I have a friend who often says to me, "Hey now, you're being pretty tough on my friend Tasha. Can you give her a break?" I am so grateful for this sweet, welcomed perspective.

And if God is willing and able to have the same kind of compassion for me, there's no reason on earth why I can't give myself a little grace when I inevitably stumble and fall.

I wish I could have learned sooner how to have compassion on myself, but becoming a parent has only reinforced this lesson for me. When my babies make a mess—and let me tell you, they make some *seriously gross* messes—my inclination isn't to shame them. My first thought is, *They're learning and growing. They're so, so small.* As soon as one mess is cleaned up, I guarantee another one's been made.

But I don't care about the mess. What I care about is my children. And if God is willing and able to have the same kind of compassion for me, there's no reason on earth why I can't give myself a little grace when I inevitably stumble and fall.

You and I are God's children, and no matter how many years we put on the clock, we'll never *stop* being His.

> For the LORD's portion is his people,
> Jacob his allotted inheritance.
> In a desert land he found him,
> in a barren and howling waste.
> He shielded him and cared for him;
> he guarded him as the apple of his eye,
> like an eagle that stirs up its nest
> and hovers over its young,
> that spreads its wings to catch them
> and carries them aloft.
> —Deuteronomy 32:9–11

QUESTIONS TO CONSIDER

1. As you take a moment to imagine God as the ultimate Father, what words come to mind to describe Him?

2. If you have children of your own or have kids in your life, what have you learned from them? What perspective have you gained from being around them?

3. Do you tend to be hard on yourself, or are you good at cutting yourself some slack? How can we better embrace the practice of forgiving ourselves, trying to do better, and then moving on?

Chapter 22

LYLA

When Levi was still little, Keith and I both found ourselves working as hard as ever professionally. Juggling a family and touring is no joke, y'all. A vacation wasn't really in the budget for us at the time, but some generous people reached out and asked if they could treat us to one.

"We've got a condo on the Jersey Shore," they said. "Would you want to stay there for a little while?"

Um, yeah!

We barely knew these folks, but we needed a break so badly and felt a peace about accepting their offer. So we packed up our baby and headed north.

When we got to the house, the fridge was fully stocked. The hosts had handwritten some of their favorite recipes for us, made a list of their favorite restaurants, and left behind a stack of gift cards. We didn't have to lift a finger to enjoy ourselves on this trip. I couldn't imagine a better example of genuine hospitality.

The Jersey Shore was the perfect place to relax and get bored for the first time in a long time. We looked at the water, rested, and rode bikes around with Levi trailing behind us in a little baby cart. It was such a sweet time for us—a much-needed respite.

One afternoon Levi was napping, and Keith was in the living room. I was praying in the bedroom, and I heard the Lord tell me to start praying for another baby. *Wow, that's a real word dropped on me*, I thought. I couldn't help but remember how everything surrounding Levi's birth had been so difficult. But I decided to tell Keith.

I stood up and started walking to the living room, but he met me in the hallway. We locked eyes, and Keith said, "I think God just told me to get into real estate."

I blinked. "Well, I think God just told me that we should start praying for another child."

That story makes me laugh even now because God was speaking to us in opposite rooms of the house. We decided to pray together right then and there, and within two months, Keith had purchased a rental property and I was pregnant with Lyla. Though Keith and I had once wondered if we'd ever have children at all, here we were being blessed with a second baby.

* * *

Despite the many gains I'd made in my relationship with God, I still found myself afraid of another long, painful, dramatic labor. Even more, I feared that our daughter would not be breathing after delivery, just like Levi. The trauma of Levi's birth still gripped me, but I knew my only choice was to trust God.

I walked through the healing prayer once again: *God, tell me where You were when I was in labor and Levi was born. Where will You be when my daughter comes into the world?* He had been there with us, and He had protected us. Slowly but surely, God healed my emotional wounds. Whatever happened to us, He would oversee it.

God had carried us through once again.

All my worries were for nothing. Compared to Levi's birth, Lyla's was straightforward, drama-free, and redemptive. I think I pushed for twelve whole minutes this time.

When she came out crying, I cried out in gratitude. God had carried us through once again.

To this day, the healing prayer practice I learned in Colorado remains a staple in my faith diet. The process reminds me of God's presence every time I listen for Him to tell me that He was, He is, and He is to come. But it's worth repeating that the practice itself is only powerful because of the One behind it: Jesus. He is the Savior who restored sight to the blind, walked on water, and raised the dead to life. And when he died and rose again, it was to save you and me. Healing comes from God and God alone.

* * *

When Lyla was about a year old, I was getting her out of her car seat to carry her through a Best Buy parking lot. I stumbled over something, and in a split second, my knees hit the ground. Though I held my daughter with a death grip, the impact when I landed forced her up and out of my arms.

I rushed her to the hospital, running every red light in my path. Then I parked on the sidewalk and grass in front of the hospital and sprinted in the door. As the doctors examined her, they found that she had a skull fracture and a brain bleed that needed to be treated. If you've ever watched your child in peril like that, you understand how I was feeling. I was in shock at what had happened, and though Lyla recovered, I was traumatized. The horror of it all made its home deep in my brain.

Fortunately, the medical professionals at Vanderbilt recommended that Keith and I schedule some counseling for ourselves. "These kinds of accidents can give parents PTSD," they said. I really appreciated them taking such good care of Lyla, and it was also wonderful that they were looking out for us as well. And as it turned out, they were right.

For months, I replayed the fall in my head. I had dreams about it that dredged up the terror and the shock. The counseling helped me grieve what happened, and as Lyla continued to be a healthy and happy child, my mind began to stabilize.

I thought I had mostly gotten over the accident when one day much later we drove past the same parking lot. Memories of that day came flooding back, and I had to park the car and fall apart. I called Keith sobbing, unsure why the feelings had come back at what felt like a heightened level. My body had likely stored up a lot of the trauma, and I just needed to release it.

Once again, I returned to the process. I prayed, *Jesus, where were You in that parking lot? What do You have to say to me right now?* I grew quiet, and I listened. Waited for His peace. He reminded me that He had been there with us and that Lyla was alive and safe. He, the Creator of the universe, is in control of every outcome. I exhaled and took solace in this simple truth.

* * *

Though counseling and therapy bore a heavy stigma of shame, I'm so grateful that both the church and secular society are opening their eyes to its importance. God is the One who saved my life, but He has used counselors and other professionals to do it. When I reflect on the major turning points behind me, I still see my time at Crossroads as a sort of apex. My counselor, Pete, was central to my healing, as he taught me how to dredge up past hurts, dwell in God's presence, and listen to Him through healing prayer. Without Pete's patience and direction, who knows where I would have wound up.

If you're interested in more about improving your mental health, I suggest you check out my other book, *Boundless: A Guided Prayer Journal to Move Freedom from*

Your Head to Your Heart. In that workbook, I go deeper with the lessons I learned at Crossroads and use my own stories to supplement those practices.

Even more, I hope you will consider whether a licensed professional could help you. If it's within your means and available to you, I suggest you give it a try. Look for counselors with credentials, and ask friends for recommendations of people they trust. And if you find yourself face to face with a counselor who makes you feel judged, ashamed, or uncomfortable, feel free to walk right out of the room and look for someone with whom you feel accepted, welcome, and safe.

And if the voice you are hearing is rude or resentful in your ears, feel free to let it pass right on by.

If you decide to try the healing prayer for yourself, can I give you just one more tip? I've discovered that I can discern God's voice from noise when His words inhabit the Bible's definition of love. If you've forgotten the definition, here it is: "Love is patient and kind; love does not envy or boast; it is not arrogant or rude. It does not insist on its own way; it is not irritable or resentful; it does not rejoice at wrongdoing, but rejoices with the truth. Love bears all things,

believes all things, hopes all things, endures all things"
(1 Corinthians 13:4–7 ESV).

Since God *is* love, I think it's safe to assume that this
is how He sounds as well. And if the voice you are hearing
is rude or resentful in your ears, feel free to let it pass right
on by. God would prefer to speak love and hope over you,
His dear child.

> *Dear friends, let us love one another, for love comes*
> *from God. Everyone who loves has been born of God*
> *and knows God. Whoever does not love does not know*
> *God, because God is love. This is how God showed his*
> *love among us: He sent his one and only Son into the*
> *world that we might live through him. This is love: not*
> *that we loved God, but that he loved us and sent his*
> *Son as an atoning sacrifice for our sins. Dear friends,*
> *since God so loved us, we also ought to love one another.*
> *No one has ever seen God; but if we love one another,*
> *God lives in us and his love is made complete in us.*
> —1 John 4:7–12

QUESTIONS TO CONSIDER

1. If you've survived a traumatic event, what have you said to God about it? Where was He when the event occurred?

2. In the past, how have you filtered God's words out from the noise? What are the hallmarks of His voice?

3. Have you ever chosen to give something that was worrying you over to God? What did it feel like when you resigned it to His care?

Chapter 23

BALANCE

Lately, my daughter loves to play with my hair. The way she rolls it between her tiny fingers is precious, though it does a real number on my strands. As I lie there with her, coaxing her to sleep, I thank God for each of these perfect, fleeting moments. I know they will not last forever.

Parenting these days is about operating on no sleep, having little privacy, doing things I don't feel like doing. . . . Sometimes all I need is five minutes of alone time, so I wind up in the bathroom for about two minutes before my kids and husband find me again. I love them more than life, but can I get a little space, please? Keith once asked me, "Why do you take such long showers?" I almost laughed in his face. If I get a twenty-minute shower once every four days, I feel blessed!

You don't need to have kids to feel this way. Maybe you have a demanding job or are caretaking for family members and wonder if you'll ever get your life in balance. I won't pretend that I have it all figured out, because even when I have other people to help me, it's still a struggle to prioritize and set boundaries. When it feels like everyone is making demands on your time—and I've yet to meet a person who doesn't feel this—it's a daily battle to figure out what matters most.

> When it feels like everyone is making demands on your time—and I've yet to meet a person who doesn't feel this—it's a daily battle to figure out what matters most.

Time is not a renewable resource. You only have so much of it, and only you will value your time in the way it deserves to be valued. Your goals may differ from mine, but I know I need space once in a while and that I need to prioritize my family. Sometimes I need to schedule that time, sometimes I can squeeze it in, and other times I need to get mad and force it. Some things can wait, and some things can't—and it's important to know which is which. Women especially aren't encouraged to set boundaries and tell people no, but this is me giving you permission to learn your limits and expect other people to respect them.

Whenever my daughter gets a certain tone in her voice or whenever my son starts climbing all over me on the couch, I know those are signs that they need more time with me. You can probably tell when your relationships need mending or attention, or you can sense when your emotional health is starting to crack. Can we agree right now that it's not OK to ignore the red flags when it comes to our priorities?

I'm a big admirer of the Smallbone family and how they do things. David and Helen Smallbone have seven adult children, many of whom are involved in the CCM industry (including Rebecca St. James and for KING & COUNTRY). Over the years, their family has turned into a full-scale ministry operation, and I have loved watching them affect lives all over the world with their music, their writing, and their messages of hope and healing. Everything they do seems to be overflowing with kindness and wisdom.

One day when Levi was teeny-tiny, I went to a brunch hosted by the Gospel Music Association. At this particular event, Helen Smallbone was the keynote speaker. She recounted stories of being a mom to seven and what it was like to travel with all of them. As overwhelmed as I was with one child, I couldn't imagine having *seven*. What in the world was her secret?

"God is the secret," she said. "And taking time for self-care." She mentioned that if a mother doesn't take some time for herself each day, she'll go crazy. That was the bit I was missing. I wasn't taking any time for myself because I didn't even see how I could. Who else would do laundry? Who else would buy the groceries? Thanks to Helen's wisdom, I've learned to balance things a little better and ask for help when I need it.

Making time for self-care, reflection, prayer, and growth for any mom is already hard. For working moms, it may feel daunting or even impossible. But I don't believe that God expects you to carry on in a way that deprives you of your needs. Jesus tells us, "Take my yoke upon you and learn from me, for I am gentle and humble in heart, and you will find rest for your souls" (Matthew 11:29). Doesn't rest sound like the most wonderful thing in the universe right now? I don't think Jesus was talking about naps here, or even that extra-hour-on-Saturday-morning kind of rest, but the sentiment of His promise remains: handing Him our burdens means a lighter load for us. And He has already taken on the entire burden of our sin—a sacrifice that guaranteed our peace once and for all.

The writer of Ecclesiastes said there's a time for everything (Ecclesiastes 3:1). Of course we need to work hard. Of course we need to handle the things we are responsible for. But we must never sacrifice *being* for *doing*. *Who* we are informs everything we do. *How* we do things is influenced by who we are— what we believe, what we stand for. The minute we forget to rest is the minute we forget we are made in God's image. Even *God* rested, remember? I'd say His example is one worth following!

> The minute we forget to rest is the minute we forget we are made in God's image.

* * *

You may be thinking, *Tasha, it's not that simple. Prioritizing and setting boundaries involves telling people no.* And you'd be right. People don't exactly like it when our no stands in the way of their yes. But if you've learned anything about my journey so far, you've probably noted that it has taken me a long time to care a little less about the opinions of others and a little more about God's will for me. We have to protect our callings and priorities because no one else will do that for us. This may turn into some uncomfortable conversations sometimes, but it is possible to set boundaries with kindness and patience. The people who believe you're trying to follow God's call will understand and respect your decisions.

So much of my life has been clouded by confusion. I've spent a lot of time in mental torment, wanting to do good things for God while also worrying about pleasing everyone in the process. Here is the secret I've learned from those years: you cannot be genuine *and* a people-pleaser. That seems like an obvious thing to write, but when you're in the middle of the struggle, it doesn't feel obvious at all. We can break our backs trying to strike a balance between what we know is right and what the loudest voices are demanding from us. How different would the world be if we each found our calling in God and let Him be the one to decide whether we're living up to it or not?

Don't hear me saying that I don't care about people. Rather, loving and serving people is what matters to me most! But loving and serving them is not the same as pleasing them. Giving too much weight to others' opinions of you forces you to compromise your authentic self—the one-of-a-kind person God made you to be. It took me way too long to learn this, but once I did, I felt like a new person. Freedom defined me, not chains. You can and should listen to people who care for you and have your best interests at heart, but the key is filtering those voices out from the noise. It is all too easy to lose track of the target when your field of vision is clouded by distraction.

Last year I was feeling a lot of pressure because I had to leave my kids behind more often than I wanted. Technical issues with our tour weren't making things any easier, but at the same time, my career seemed to be building momentum. I wanted to take advantage of doors opening but not at the expense of my job as a mom. Balance seemed beyond my grasp, especially at home.

Then I had another "Smallbone moment." (Yes, this chapter is dedicated to the Smallbones. I'm a super-fan.) My husband and I were having coffee with David Smallbone, and I told him about my struggles keeping things together at home *and* on the road. "Running errands and doing chores are my responsibilities at home and leading the ministry is also up to me," I told him. "But I don't feel like I'm doing either well right now."

David looked at me and said, point-blank, "Tasha, would you rather clean your house or write a song that changes the world?"

Well, when you put it that way!

That conversation changed my life because it reminded me that we're all mere mortals here, and my job is to figure out how my time is best spent. Running errands and taking care of my home are important tasks, and they must be done. But there's no shame in asking for help when I have something more pressing or of eternal value to do.

I realize that asking and paying for help is a privilege not everyone can afford, and most of my life I was not able to hire help. I'm forever indebted to the people who help me keep the ship running from day-to-day. But my point here is to give you permission to keep some things close and let others go. Those choices and unique priorities belong to you alone. I can almost guarantee that each of you has something eating up your time that you could release: a club, a committee . . . anything you're not passionate about that absorbs your energy and takes away from things you care about more. If you take stock of your schedule and there's

> Your life won't automatically become what you want it to be; demands on your time and energy will keep coming for you until your final days.

not enough time for loved ones and your own self-care, look for ways to change it. Ask God to reveal to you if there are things you can let go of.

Your life won't automatically become what you want it to be; demands on your time and energy will keep coming for you until your final days. But you don't have to despair over it. Be intentional about what matters most to you, and with God's blessing, you'll find the balance you crave.

* * *

During seminary I lived in a condo in Encino. It was a beautiful area next a park, and I loved that it was less of a concrete jungle on that side of the valley. I drove past the park every day on my way to school and always thought to myself, *Oh, how nice. Isn't it great that people take time to walk in the park?*

One day I had a revelation about my passing thought: Deep down I believed that I was the kind of person who takes time out to enjoy the park, but I wasn't. I wasn't a person in the park! Instead, I was the person rushing down the road *watching* the people in the park. I wanted so badly to be the person who walked in the park, who enjoyed life, who simply *lived.*

I decided the very next day that I would make some adjustments and walk in the park on a regular basis. The day I began, all of the cherry trees were blooming. The tender, tiny petals lined the edges of the walkways. As I walked through what seemed like a fairytale, I heard a voice saying, *Spring is coming. There are blossoms on the tree of your life, Tasha. Don't give up now.* My quiet time and the beauty of the blossoms served as a reminder that the fruit of my labors would indeed come.

Working is not living. Working and "getting things done" are parts of life, but they are not who we are. If we aren't intentional about listening for God, we can spend our entire lives being held hostage by what others think of us and not pursuing the things we are meant for. We can either become obsessed with how we are perceived, or we can get buried under the weight of opinions that don't line up with what God wants for our lives. I have spent too much time feeling trapped, and I don't want that for you. I want us to feel emboldened and free—full of joy knowing that God's will is perfect and good. An abiding peace comes with knowing God is working on our behalf at all times, no matter how we are spending our time. He is bigger than all of it.

Let's protect our time and our rest. I promise you will never regret the choices you made that opened up more space for God to do His work in you.

Come to me, all you who are weary and burdened,
and I will give you rest. Take my yoke upon you
and learn from me, for I am gentle and humble
in heart, and you will find rest for your souls.
For my yoke is easy and my burden is light.
—Matthew 11:28–30

QUESTIONS TO CONSIDER

1. Do you feel that your day-to-day life reflects your priorities and makes time for rest? If not, what could you do today to change your routine or schedule?
2. Describe a moment when you felt guilty for saying no or setting a boundary. Was your decision the right one?
3. Remember that God Himself rested on the seventh day of creation! Why do you think we tend to overwork and overextend ourselves to the detriment of our much-needed health?

Chapter 24

LOOK WHAT YOU'VE DONE

Since that moment when I was thirteen and answered an early call to ministry, all I wanted for my life was to help people and do something for God. I didn't know that I would wind up getting to do this amazing job that I love. For so many years, I wandered and wondered about my specific purpose. Each step on the road is different from the last, but I'm so grateful to be able to look around right now and say to God, *You've done all of this. You brought me here, and only You could have done it.* He walked with me through the early days, He rescued my heart and mind, He opened doors, and He even saved my life. It's just icing on the cake that He's willing to use me to share His message of love, forgiveness, and freedom with the people I meet day to day. To be used by Him like this is all I've ever wanted.

I received the kindest letter recently from a woman who first heard my music on the radio. Like me, she'd been in a place where hope was dwindling, but God had mercifully rescued her from the darkness. Her generous spirit was so present in her writing, and the fact that a song broadcast across airwaves had connected us felt almost like a miracle.

In her letter, she shared with me the words from Galatians 5:13: "You, my brothers and sisters, were called to be free. But do not use your freedom to indulge the flesh; rather, serve one another humbly in love." Her chosen scripture touched me so deeply because that is exactly what I want to do with my life, and that is exactly how I want you to feel: *free in Christ Jesus.*

What does freedom look like for you? For me, it's how God has taken the things that made me weak as a kid and turned them into my strengths. I never, ever thought that would happen, and I want everyone to feel the kind of confidence and peace I've discovered as I listen to God and follow His voice. As I've learned to trust Him with my heart and my life, I've learned that He loves the real me, not some photoshopped version that looks good on a concert promo. He's promised to be with me all the way, and He's promised to be there for you. He loves us, He wants good things for us, and He is with us. Praise God for what He has done and what He will do.

When I perform on the road, I get to meet incredible people from every corner of the country. I also receive messages from folks all over the world who want to tell me what God has done for them. Other people share with me that my music has helped them get through difficult things: losing children and parents, recovering from trauma, losing their health, you name it. Listeners tell me they need the hope and the reminder of God's closeness. I need

> As I've learned to trust Him with my heart and my life, I've learned that He loves the real me, not some photoshopped version that looks good on a concert promo.

those things, too, which is why I wrote those songs! What a blessing to share them with you and know that we are together on this journey with Him.

If you're familiar with my music, I want you to know that the lyrics I sing are reflections of my heart. They are honest reckonings and sincere words of praise. As you no doubt have figured out by now, I'm not afraid of asking God the hard questions and waiting in silence for His answers. When Keith and I started writing music together, our goal was to praise God and tell the truth about the Christian life, which no one guaranteed would be easy. But Jesus did promise to be with us, and I take great solace in that. My hope is for you to connect with God through my music, to find peace and comfort in His abundance and His power. He really has done so much, and He's not done yet.

"Look What You've Done" is not only the name of one of my songs; it's also the theme of my life. It captures how God has taken my broken pieces and made them whole. God has also blessed me beyond measure and given me experiences and adventures I will never forget, but those are all secondary to the power of His saving grace. So I sing to Him:

Look what You've done
Look what You've done in me
You spoke Your truth into the lies I let my heart
believe
Look at me now
Look how You made me new
The enemy did everything that he could do
Oh but look what You've done

On the cross, in a grave
With a stone, rolled away
All my debt, it was paid
Look what You've done

In my heart, in my mind
In my soul, in my life
With my hands lifted high
I'm singing
Look what You've done

God can do all of this for you and more. He's already sent His Son to save you; now it's your choice to accept His gifts and welcome the one-of-a-kind life He has planned for you. I want you to be able to look in the mirror and say, "Wow, God, You are so strong in me, and You love me just the way I am." The feeling of knowing God adores you and is in control provides a freedom like no other.

Knowing God is present with us gives us incomparable courage and joy. He can heal every wound and infuse every tender part of us with strength. And after searching all over the world for answers to my soul's questions, I can say with confidence that no other god can do that. Jesus is unmatched in His willingness to love, forgive, and bless. And He is willing to welcome you home again and again, every single time.

I want to leave you with this prayer: May God's divine, eternal, abundant peace surround you and radiate into the lives of everyone in your orbit. May He heal your broken heart and remind you of His everlasting, promised presence. May you find yourself able to look at your circumstances and find God's handprints all over them. And may each day be filled with joy, wonder, and reminders that you are beloved by the Father whose kingdom reigns forevermore. Amen.

> May God's divine, eternal, abundant peace surround you and radiate into the lives of everyone in your orbit.

So in Christ Jesus you are all children of God through faith, for all of you who were baptized into Christ have clothed yourselves with Christ. There is neither Jew nor Gentile, neither slave nor free, nor is there male and female, for you are all one in Christ Jesus. If you belong to Christ, then you are Abraham's seed, and heirs according to the promise.
—Galatians 3:26–29

QUESTIONS TO CONSIDER

1. What has God done in your life that you want to tell others about? What do you still hope for Him to do?

2. What can you be honest with God about today that you may have never been honest about before?

3. Who in your life needs to be reminded of God's presence? Who needs to be reminded that they are loved?

ACKNOWLEDGMENTS

To my husband—without your sacrifice I couldn't do what I do. You've encouraged my calling from the very beginning.

To Levi and Lyla—I pray you always know the God of this story and that He's ever present in your own. Everything in life up until this point has prepared me to be your mother, and I am grateful for you.

To the FCM family—Mike, Brandi, Dave, and Kacie—you figuratively keep my world spinning! You are a force full of heart, skill, and wisdom.

To the EMF family—thank you for helping reach the world with all you do.

ABOUT THE AUTHOR

TASHA LAYTON is a contemporary Christian musician who finds her identity and purpose in her personal relationship with Jesus. Layton's musical career took off with her appearance on Season 9 of *American Idol* and during the four years she spent touring as a back-up vocalist for pop superstar Katy Perry.

In 2020, Layton was first named one of *Billboard's* Top 5 female Christian artists of the year on the heels of her breakthrough single "Into The Sea (It's Gonna Be OK)." Now, her 2021 smash hit "Look What You've Done" is testifying on radio stations across the country to the incredible transformation she's experienced after moving God's truth from her head to her heart.

Tasha has experienced the depths of suicidal thoughts, struggling with comparison and self-worth. But her God brought her through and set her course toward a life of joy, freedom, boldness, and eternal perspective. Today, she blesses people everywhere with her breathtaking talents and testimony.

From humble beginnings in small-town South Carolina, to far off places on almost every continent, Tasha has experienced God's love every step of the way. In 2022, she launched her new online show, *Boundless,* with K-LOVE OnDemand. Publishing in 2023, *Look What You've Done: The Lies We Believe & The Truth That Sets Us Free* is her first book.

Keep in touch with
Tasha at:
tashalayton.com

or on socials at

facebook.com/tasha.layton
instagram.com/tashalayton
twitter.com/TLLayton